ONE WEEK
LOAN

Counselling in Practice

Series editor: Windy Dryden
Associate editor: E. Thomas Dowd

Counselling in Practice is a series of books developed especially for counsellors and students of counselling which provides practical, accessible guidelines for dealing with clients with specific, but very common, problems.

Counselling Couples

Donald L. Bubenzer
& John D. West

SAGE Publications
London • Thousand Oaks • New Delhi

First published 1993
Reprinted 1994

SAGE Publications Ltd
6 Bonhill Street
London EC2A 4PU

SAGE Publications Inc
2455 Teller Road
Thousand Oaks, California 91320

SAGE Publications India Pvt Ltd
32, M-Block Market
Greater Kailash – I
New Delhi 110 048

British Library Cataloguing in Publication Data

Bubenzer, Donald
    Counselling Couples. – (Counselling in Practice Series)
    I. Title   II. West, John   III. Series
    361.3

    ISBN 0–8039–8420–0
    ISBN 0–8039–8421–9 pbk

Library of Congress catalog card number 93–083563

Typeset by Mayhew Typesetting, Rhayader, Powys
Printed and bound in Great Britain by
Biddles Ltd, Guildford and King's Lynn

Contents

Preface

Our understanding of couples counselling comes from our study in the field, our interactions with colleagues and students, and our practice as counsellors. As a result, we see ourselves as students of marital and family counselling and are in deep appreciation of those teachers, colleagues, students, and clients who have been stimulating and supportive in our studies.

In practice, as in this book, we focus on identifying patterns of interaction in relationships, facilitating the couple's awareness of these patterns, and challenging unproductive patterns and supporting alternative behaviors and understandings when couples become stuck in less than satisfying relationships. Often, the cases we have presented in this book are not based on any one couple but reflect a blend of the issues we have encountered as counsellors, and in each illustration an effort has been made to protect the anonymity of the couple. It would be our hope that, as she or he reads this book, the reader will begin to think about the couples in her or his counselling practice. Specifically, we hope the reader would consider patterns of interacting in relationships, interventions that might facilitate an awareness of patterns, and interventions that might interrupt unproductive sequences and that might facilitate alternative patterns. If our remarks become a stimulus for developing interventions suited for the reader's counselling cases, rather than becoming a list of possible techniques, we will feel that this book has served its purpose.

Furthermore, we are most grateful for the clerical assistance provided by Linda Fosnight in preparing this manuscript. Of course, as we grow older we are also aware that our study and lives as counsellors are integrally related to our own lives as family members. Minuchin and Fishman (1981) noted that we all belong to different familial subsystems, and we would suggest that life in these family units can be viewed as interesting, meaningful, and complex. For instance, we are sons to our parents and brothers to our siblings and we are husbands to our wives and fathers to our children, so, like many folks, we play multiple roles within our families. The moments when we reflect on our family units are indeed enjoyable and help us to surface the deep appreciation we have for the patience, support, and stimulation provided by Nancy and Eileen who, among their other roles, are our partners in life.

Note

British spelling is used in the preliminary pages and running heads and American spelling and punctuation are used throughout the text. 'Couple' is treated as a plural noun.

1

The Nature of Couple Relationships

To write about the counseling of couples is to assume that the dyadic relationship is a significant social unit and to assume that the well-being of couples has impact for our way of life. Indeed, counselors who report couples counseling as a part of their case-load and as a part of their repertoire of skills view this dyadic unit as a core social relationship. For example, of the United States residents in 1989 who were 15 years of age and older, 55.7% were married and living with their spouse, 17.9% were married but separated, widowed or divorced, and only 26.4% were never married (US Bureau of the Census, 1990). Furthermore, Glick and Spanier (1980) have indicated there has been a substantial increase of unmarried cohabiting couples in the United States, and they mentioned an increase from 530,000 couples in 1970 to 1,137,000 couples in 1978. In Britain in 1981, 8% of single women were cohabiting; in 1988/9 the figure was 16% (Office of Population and Censuses Surveys [OPCS], 1991). As a result, it would seem appropriate to conclude that an interest in the coupling life style certainly exists.

Further clarification of the trends for couples indicates that in 1970 the median age for men to marry in the United States was 23.2 years and for women it was 20.8 years, while by 1989 the median age for men had increased to 26.2 years of age and for women it had increased to 23.8 years (US Bureau of the Census, 1990). In addition, Lauer and Lauer reported 'an increasing number of women are delaying having their first child until their mid- or even late thirties' (1991: 10). This would suggest that couples are waiting both longer to marry and longer to have children. Moreover, Census Bureau figures indicated that the proportion of married women who were employed increased from 30.5% in 1960 to 56.5% in 1988 (US Bureau of the Census, 1990). A dramatic increase also occurred for women who had children between 6 and 17 years of age (39.0% employed in 1960 and 72.5% employed in 1988) and for women who had children under 6 years of age (18.6% employed in 1960 and 57.1% employed in 1988). In Britain in 1981, 25% of women with children under five were in employment, a quarter of them full-time. By 1989 the figures had risen to 41%, with about one-third full-time. In 1989, half of all married women worked full-time (OPCS, 1991). Indeed, it appears that the nature of marriage is changing.

Marriages are also complex in terms of the number of times people have been married and the differences in marriage patterns that occur when age and gender are considered. The National Center for Health Statistics (1988) noted that in 1987 there were about one half as many divorces (1,157,000) as there were marriages (2,421,000). From reviews of studies pertaining to marriage and divorce, Hacker (1983) reported the median length of marriage at divorce as 6.8 years and noted 73% of divorced persons remarry, while Spanier and Glick (1980) reported the median time between divorce and remarriage at about three years. Hacker (1983) also observed a discrepancy in the proportions for men and women who remarry after divorce: ages 30–35, 52.5% of the men and 44.8% of the women; ages 35–44, 57.9% of the men and 42.1% of the women; ages 45–54, 61.9% of the men and 38.1% of the women; ages 55–64, 67.6% of the men and 32.4% of the women; and ages 65 and up, 74.4% of the men and 25.6% of the women. As a consequence of the number of persons marrying, remarrying, and cohabiting, we would again suggest that although the portrait of marriage is changing, there does seem to be a strong interest in the coupling life style.

In addition to the demographic information presented above, counselors have rated marital difficulties as the most prevalent problem presented by clients (Bubenzer, Zimpfer, & Mahrle, 1990). Consequently, with the preference for marrying or a coupling life style and with the frequency of marital difficulty, counselors are continually looking for material to assist them in better understanding couple relationships. For the purposes of this book, we will be discussing couples as dyadic relationships in which two parties expect to have a long-term intimate commitment. Obviously, coupling takes many forms other than the traditional spousal unit (for instance, remarried couples, cohabiting couples, and gay and lesbian couples); however, our examples will come largely from the realm of marital relationships. We do believe, however, that the targets and techniques of the interventions discussed in this book also apply to other dyadic relationships. Before looking at the typical areas in which couples encounter difficulty, let's spend some time considering characteristics of couple relationships.

1   Voluntary nature of coupling

2   Balance in the couple's relationship

3   Temporal aspects of coupling

4   Merging of systems as part of coupling

5   Giving and receiving of support as part of coupling

6   Maintaining of separateness and individuality in coupling

Figure 1.1   *Variables characteristic of couple relationships*

Variables Characteristic of Couple Relationships

The couple relationship is in some ways quite different from all other dyadic units, and we believe that six variables are characteristic of coupling (see Figure 1.1). When taken individually these variables are not necessarily unique to an intimate partnership but, when considered as a group, they do seem to be part of the coupling process. These variables will be directly or indirectly referred to in many of our remarks, case examples, and illustrations.

Voluntary Nature of Coupling

The rising divorce rate has highlighted the voluntary nature of dyadic relationships. People often say, 'Once you're a parent you're always a parent but marriage is voluntary.' As an aside, we know that some parents also see that role as voluntary. Those of us in the counseling field know that the voluntary nature of marriages is not as apparent as divorce data, 'quickie' divorces, or disillusionment procedures would lead some to believe. Frequently, women will indicate that they stay in their marriages because they fear what would happen to them physically and/or financially if they filed for a divorce. Moreover, at one period, some thought their only avenue to sex was marriage and with the rise of sexually transmitted diseases people may again believe that monogamy is safe even if not satisfying. As a result, even with our emphasis on disposable items, society seems to press for the marital relationship. Ultimately, however, marriage is voluntary and frequently the biggest leaps forward come when one or both parties realize that they do not have to be married. At times this realization leads to divorce while at other times it leads to both parties taking their relationship more seriously.

Balance in the Couple's Relationship

Goldenberg and Goldenberg (1990) suggested that family systems, which would include the couple subsystem, required that members maintain both a stable and steady pattern or routine for relating to one another and the ability to change their pattern or routine when conditions require. Often challenges to stability or homeostasis come at times when the couple is going through a life transition, such as when a partner becomes pregnant or retires. During these periods some instability exists in the relationship until a new pattern of relating to one another is developed (a new balance) or until the old way of doing things is again seen as being satisfactory (the old balance). With the example of retirement, a new balance might be observed if the retiring person and her or his partner reallocate responsibilities and become involved in a new set of activities outside the home. An example of the old balance continuing might occur when a retiring mate takes on a new career and the partner also maintains her or his traditional roles. In order to maintain a productive balance in the relationship, the couple will at times need to engage in some change and at other times rely on routines or accustomed patterns of interacting that provide for stability in the relationship.

Too much stability, however, restricts opportunities for growth and too much flexibility or change can be associated with chaos and little in the way of agreed-upon expectations for the relationship. It is not unusual for couples in counseling to describe a sense of hopelessness that leads the counselor to think that the relationship is way out of balance. Sometimes, however, what appears to be a minor change in the relationship can actually restore the system to an appropriate balance. This is true in part because the couple's judgment about what constitutes a successful therapeutic outcome may differ significantly from what the counselor might think needs to happen for the couple. The exuberance of a novice counselor may suggest that a couple's relationship requires a 'major overhaul' while, in fact, the couple may move on with their life together after a 'minor tune up.' Also, overstatement of a problem is sometimes characteristic of couples early in counseling and, perhaps, this can be viewed as an expression of their frustration at being unable to resolve recurrent problems.

Temporal Aspects of Coupling

The couple relationship also has a temporal component. That is, an intimate relationship not only assumes a here-and-now or current focus to the relationship, but also has a history and a future. It seems to us that histories of successful problem resolution lead couples to a stronger sense of their ability to handle a variety of life events, while a history of failures at negotiating problems leads to a level of discouragement in the relationship which curtails individual growth as well as further development of the relationship. Similarly, the couple's ability to conceptualize a future and to plan for a life together provides an essential ingredient for binding the relationship during periods of change and instability. So, indeed, temporal aspects of an intimate partnership become important for understanding the couple relationship.

Merging of Systems as Part of Coupling
The formation of the couple relationship always involves the merging of at least two systems with differing values, emotional levels, ways of thinking and ways of behaving. Someone has said that the wedding vows should be to 'love, honor and negotiate.' The negotiation process is about doing things 'my way,' 'your way,' or 'our way.' Each partner in a relationship enters with a view of reality based upon unquestioned assumptions. These assumptions are often established in one's family of origin and revolve around issues like the couple's religious affiliations, political positions, biases for urban or rural living, and thoughts on the importance of education. For example, early in marriage, couples are almost daily bumping into family skeletons that suggest what to eat, when to eat, what soap to use, how to hang clothes, who is supposed to run the vacuum and when, and whose folks we need to visit and for how long. When one considers all of the decisions and adjustments that are made early in the life of a couple's relationship, it is sometimes surprising that any relationship survives. Even when a couple come for counseling they have often not begun to question the assumptions that underpin their views of how life should be lived. In times of crises, conflict around the 'right' way of doing things re-emerges and some issues get rehashed. Indeed, the merging of two systems is a process that continues throughout the lifespan.

Giving and Receiving of Support as Part of Coupling
Family systems counselors are often asking themselves, 'What's the function of the couple relationship?' We tend to view a chief function of the couple relationship as that of providing support. That is, partners in the relationship expect to receive support and need to learn to provide support. Support occurs during those times when help is needed in bearing up under the pressures of a demanding job, needy neighbors, obnoxious children, or any of a variety of perceived loses or challenges.

Being able to provide support requires consideration of one's partner when making decisions about one's individual life and the family. It does not mean giving up one's own life to bring fulfillment to one's partner, but considering one's partner and learning to accommodate to them in the choices that are made is important. To a large extent, it's the ability to consider one's partner that helps one to transcend self and to grow as a person and as a couple. We would suggest that growth as a couple and as an individual are often interrelated and that transcending oneself, through considering one's partner, also facilitates individual growth and development. The ability to take one's partner into consideration in making daily decisions is related to Alfred Adler's (Ansbacher & Ansbacher, 1956) notion of social interest. This function of a couple's relationship, to receive and provide support, is seen in the full breadth of the couple's life together; for instance, in each partner's willingness to be sensitive to vocational aspirations, wishes for intimacy, desires for social contact, and longing for time separate from the relationship. Indeed, the ability to provide and receive support is a primary function of an intimate relationship and, thus, is also a characteristic of the relationship.

Maintaining of Separateness and Individuality in Coupling

Finally, the ability of the couple to appreciate each other's desire for individuality or separateness from the partnership is an important characteristic in developing a relationship. At first glance this may appear to be paradoxical, but couples do need to maintain some boundaries, some separateness in order to pursue and develop individual interests. Friedman (1990) stated that partners separate because they are unable to be separate. This ability to see oneself and one's partner as belonging to the relationship and, at the same time, being separate from the relationship often requires continual effort. It also requires that each partner have a level of personal security about the stability of the relationship. The tricky part here is in striking an appropriate amount of togetherness and separateness so that each member's sense of belonging is preserved but without sacrificing one's individuality.

Obviously, the willingness to encourage a partner's individual development of thoughts, feelings, and behaviors can occur in any number of arenas. These may include the development of political or religious involvement, the frequency and type of contact with one's extended family or friendship networks, as well as the infinite number of thoughts and feelings that surround daily encounters. Rather than a desire for individuality and separateness from one's partner being the antithesis of an intimate relationship, striking an acceptable blend of these variables is viewed as an important characteristic of coupling.

Typical Areas of Symptom Formation in Couple Relationships

Opinion concerning the nature of client problems varies among counselors. Some view the behavior that clients bring as being the area of needed adjustment while others see client behavior as symptomatic of underlying issues that need to be resolved. In either instance, behavior or perspective, complaints reflect a discrepancy between how at least one member of the couple experiences the relationship and how that member would like to see it. Several writers (Knox, 1971; Markman et al., 1988) have indicated that ten areas are among those commonly presented by couples in the counselor's office (see Figure 1.2).

1	Economic issues	6	Relationships with extended family
2	Companionship–intimacy	7	Religion
3	Work and recreation	8	Friends
4	Parenting	9	Substance abuse
5	Household chores	10	Communication

Figure 1.2 *Typical areas of symptom formation in couple relationships*

Economic Issues
Money matters show up frequently as a problem area. Usually the issue centers around how one or both parties spend money. If the problem is jointly owned by the couple the solution is more easily reached. When one or both parties blame the other for their financial inadequacy anger usually rises and trust diminishes. We once worked with a case where the couple were married for six months before the wife realized that her husband was not employed. They both left home in the morning and arrived home again at night at regular and reasonable times. The marital agreement was that he handled financial matters and she turned her paycheck over to him faithfully. As time went on, however, bill collectors began to

appear at their door and finally, after having her suspicions aroused, she obtained a bank statement and found that only her check was being deposited. Further inquiry revealed that her husband was not hiding his check elsewhere. He simply was not earning a paycheck. Not only was she faced with a lack of economic security but the issue of trust was damaged beyond repair. Not all issues of economic security are this bizarre or severe but most raise issues about how decisions are made and who makes decisions about spending money.

Companionship–Intimacy

It has been stated that there are two great books that will enable you to fully understand relationships. One is the couple's check-book and the other is their appointment book. How people spend their money and how people spend their time are two revealing indices of personal values. The issue of time often gets translated into companionship issues for couples. One partner may be concerned about how much time their spouse spends with them versus how much time they spend with friends, parents, children, etc. The other partner may feel, however, that the nature of the time spent together is more important than the amount of time. With regard to intimacy, client concerns may revolve around the frequency of sexual activity as well as who is allowed to initiate sexual activity. For example, it is not unusual to hear one partner complain that the other does not know how to be intimate without sexual inter-course, that only one partner feels the freedom to initiate intimate and/or sexual contact, or that intimacy and/or sexual contact is reserved for late at night on a particular day of the week or month. Often an expressed discrepancy between the amount and kind of time spent together is a reflection of the question, 'Do you care about or love me?'

Work and Recreation

During other periods, issues for couples revolve around how much time is spent at work and how much time is spent in recreation. The latter issue will often be expressed as, 'We have nothing in common.' Certainly many couples have little in common and they are perfectly happy. But when difficulties arise, it seems that 'we have nothing in common' or 'we've grown apart from each other' is viewed as an acceptable rationale for getting a divorce. Spouses will, at times, also complain because their partner spends too much time at work. Examples of these problems may include the spouse who complains that her or his mate spends half of each weekend at the office, or that her or his partner brings work home from the office each evening and has become a stranger in the relationship. Again, complaints about these time commitments are usually masking the question, 'Do you love me?' or 'Do you care about me?' They can also reflect an unasked question on the part of a complainant, 'Are you having an affair?'

Concerns about recreation are expressed in terms of time spent and the kinds of activities pursued. Grievances about recreation may start with the honeymoon. We once worked with a couple, married twenty years, who still fought over how satisfactory their honeymoon had been. They had gone camping and fishing and the wife had been quite offended but said nothing at the time. Again, resentments pertaining to how free time is spent may mask the concern that 'If you loved me, you'd be willing to give more consideration to my interests.'

Parenting

Members of a dyad will often have complaints about how much of a burden childcare has become for one or both. Typically, spouses who report differences in the area of parenting present issues like the preferred number and spacing of children, the time each partner spends with children, the discipline of children, or the kinds of activities in which children should participate. It is common that the partner who is more concerned about parenting also becomes overinvolved with parenting and, at the same time, their spouse then becomes the peripheral parent. On the other hand, spouses may be so competitive that each believes only she or he has the right answer to parenting issues and parenting then becomes a fertile ground for power struggles in the couple's relationship. Indeed, it would seem that parenting styles can reflect the quality of a couple's relationship. One couple entered the counselor's office complaining that their adolescent son was out of control. As the issue was explored, it was discovered that both parents agreed on setting consequences for the boy's inappropriate behavior, but the one who was left with enforcing the discipline would renege on holding to the consequences when the other partner moved back into a peripheral position in their relationship. It was this ineffective but overinvolved and peripheral parenting style that prevented the establishment of an effective parenting unit.

Household Chores

The couple may present themselves in the counselor's office with complaints about the division of household chores. Often what we find is that one partner has become over-responsible while the other has become more removed from those chores that need to be accomplished to keep the home running efficiently. For instance, one partner might be found making certain that bills are paid, meals are prepared, cleaning is completed, and home maintenance is accomplished. It is important to note that when one partner becomes over-responsible, even if the peripheral mate pitches in to equalize the work, it can occur that the over-responsible one will be so critical of the other's efforts that she or he returns to being over-responsible while the mate once again becomes peripheral. At times, it seems as though the couple's historical patterns of inter-action supersede individual desires to change the allocation of household chores.

As an illustration, it is not difficult to imagine one partner setting aside weekends for softball games or golf outings while the other becomes over-involved in home maintenance. Perhaps after a fair amount of complaining our 'athlete' decides to help tackle the list of weekend chores. As this partner pitches in with vacuum-ing, laundry and gardening, she or he is criticized for not being thorough enough, for failing to select appropriate water temperatures for the wash, and for planting the begonias too close together. Not surprisingly, these exchanges lead the over-responsible partner to think that it may be easier to handle the chores alone while the 'athlete' begins to long for the comfort of the golf course and softball field. Such exchanges can be associated with the over- and under-responsible split that characterizes the conflict some couples experience around household chores.

Relationships with Extended Family

The couple's concerns with the extended family often revolve around the frequency of contact with extended family members and the level of influence the extended family has on the couple's efforts to develop their own relationship. Complaints about either of these issues can come from both members of the relationship or they often surface from one member with the other feeling helpless to bring about desired changes. Often the attacked partner responds by defending the behavior and requests of the extended family members. For instance, one partner might complain that the other seeks parental advice too often on decisions that affect their rela-tionship. Instead, the complainant would like the partner to solicit her or his opinion on issues affecting the two of them. Or, each member of the relationship might accuse the other of squandering away their free time with visits to the extended family. Partners may feel that scheduling more time for their relationship would take time away from visits with the extended family and, consequently, each may feel that initiating time for their relationship would be tantamount to being disloyal to the larger family. In either case, partners often have difficulty understanding why their companion cannot break free from ties with the extended family and why they do not devote more time to their relationship. Again, it seems spouses are asking each other, 'Do you love me?'

Religion

If religion is an area of symptom formation for a couple, it will often arise at the developmental juncture where the couple begin to assume responsibility for the religious training of their children. Prior to this stage of family development religious differences tend to be seen by the couple as just differences. The differences are tolerated because they have little impact on the couple. Under the watchful eye of children, parents begin to take their responsibility for moral and spiritual development more seriously. If there are religious differences between the spouses, the developmental moment sets the stage for a power struggle over religion. This struggle may take the form of deciding which religious perspective is correct, which of the spouses is more devout, which religion is the one the children will be raised in, how much money to give to the church or how to observe religious holidays. As with all symptom areas, there is a couple dynamic that underlies the issue of religion. Initially conflict over religious involvement may spring from a concern for family development but, if allowed to continue, the conflict may become a struggle for power and control. That is, the struggle may be associated with who will make the decisions in the relationship. The notion of power and control in relationships is one that has been addressed at some length by Jay Haley (1963).

Friends

Couples can also struggle over the issue of friends. Friends are often a symptomatic area during early stages of marriage. The issue arises as a reflection of the accommodation that takes place between the new mates. As the two systems merge there are questions about whose friends are better, how much time can be spent with friends and, at times, the gender of friends. Spouses will occasionally be offended by the intimacies that are shared with friends. Embarrassment and anger may be found between spouses when one or the other has shared 'private' information with friends or when more intimacy seems to be present outside rather than within the marital relationship. Friendships can also arise as a problem in later-stage marriages. Usually, these problems reflect the belief on the part of a spouse that their partner spends too much time in a recreational pursuit such as golf or that the partner has too close a relationship with a member of the opposite sex. In all these instances it seems that the importance of the marriage is being questioned.

Substance Abuse

The symptomatic area of substance abuse is today particularly problematic for both couples and counselors. Couples often have a difficult time admitting that substance abuse is occurring and that it is a problem. Counselors also have a difficult time helping the spouses see that substance abuse is a problem. As previously noted, Haley (1963) discussed the issue of power in relationships, who will be most influential, and substance use may become a very powerful 'chip' in power struggle games that couples play around a variety of issues. Issues that arise around the use of alcohol and other substances include: what and how much use is acceptable; what amount of money can be spent on the substance; what behaviors can be expected of the user and partner (such as parenting, socializing, and maintaining a job); and what behaviors won't be tolerated (such as fighting, flirting, and driving while intoxicated). Because marital counselors can be caught in the dilemma of whether or not to treat the couple for marital concerns without first dealing with the substance use problem, they may wish to use referrals to substance use specialists to assist in the treatment of the couple.

Communication

Almost all couples who come for counseling indicate that communication is a problem. They may say 'We never talk' or 'We have nothing to talk about.' Sometimes they complain that the other never has anything nice to say or that the other isn't willing to take time to talk. When they are particularly angry they may complain that the other is too mundane to talk with. Couples with communication problems usually do not use their listening skills. They are more interested in being heard than they are in listening. Actually, a reciprocal process may be observed when one focuses on being heard. That is, as one feels one isn't being listened to, one may make an extra effort to express oneself. The more one works at being heard and sacrifices listening, the more one's mate may experience not being heard and, as a result, back off from listening and concentrate on sending messages. Although couples seldom lack communication skills, they may have lost the will to engage in both the sending and receiving aspects of the communication process. Their motivation to communicate in helpful ways may have diminished and they may have developed habits of communicating in recriminating ways.

The Underlying Problem

Marital problems may be presented in one or more of the ten areas discussed above. To satisfy the couple it is usually prudent for the counselor to acknowledge and address the problems presented. If the problems presented by the couple are not addressed, the counselor has to convince the couple that what they thought was the problem is not really the issue. Although such an approach can be successful, it will often result in the development of resistance on the part of the couple. In a way, the counselor has insulted the couple by telling them they do not know what they are talking about.

At the same time that the counselor accepts the problem, as defined by the couple, as being a legitimate concern and the target of intervention, she or he also recognizes that the problem underlying the symptom revolves around how the couple relates to one another. It is their way of relating that also becomes the target of intervention. The symptom area, money, friends, etc., becomes the mechanism for evaluating the progress in couples counseling.

Tools for Relationship Satisfaction

We have found that counselors have three major avenues in assisting couples to develop more satisfying relationships. Counselors help couples (a) in renewing their sense of hope and motivation, (b) in developing ways of thinking about their problems and relationship that are growth-producing, and (c) in developing and using the behavioral skills necessary for having a satisfying relationship. We term these three avenues of assistance: motivation, meaning, and management.

Concepts related to motivation, meaning and management have been described by many writers as being important aspects of effective functioning (see Figure 1.3). Antonovsky (1979, 1987) introduced the concept of a 'sense of coherence' as having explanatory power in terms of defining those people who are better able to adapt to stress. He indicated that people who have a strong sense of coherence view life as (a) being challenging and worth the effort, (b) being predictable and explainable, and (c) containing resources for meeting various demands. We would see having motivation to meet the challenges of a relationship as inextricably tied to having hope for the relationship and as necessary for dyadic satisfaction. Moreover, for us, establishing a sense of meaning about life suggests that the couple are able to see some structure and predictability in life that leads to healthy development. Finally, couples also appear to need behavioral management skills to negotiate the

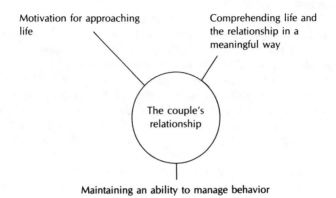

Figure 1.3   *Tools for relationship satisfaction*

intimate nature of their relationship. So, it seems that motivation, meaning and management are all important tools for relationship satisfaction.

Differing forms of the motivation, meaning and management concepts have been addressed by other writers and researchers. Pelletier (1981) wrote about a prolonged and productive involvement in family and community, an acquired status of maturity and wisdom and a pervasive sense of meaning and purpose as being important to adaptation and fulfillment in life. Kobasa (1979) found that commitment, control and challenge were three variables characteristic of hardy people, that is, people who are not filled by the stresses in life. These people seem to have much in common with those whom Adler (1964) described as having high social interest, a sense of connectedness between human beings and a willingness to cooperate with others for the common good. Additional studies (Bulman & Wortman, 1977; Ducette & Keane, 1984) have demonstrated that finding meaning in life, particularly positive meaning, has an influence on the psychological and physical health enjoyed by people. Markman (1981) found that distressed couples and nondistressed couples pay attention to different aspects of communication. Relatedly, they have different ways of making meaning.

It would seem to us then that the abovementioned authors have hinted at one or more of the tools we think couples need in order to find satisfaction in their relationship. That is, our experiences have led us to believe that counselors need to consider the couple's level of motivation for facing life, the meaning they place on life events, and the behavioral management skills they utilize while negotiating their relationship. Indeed, it is not that some couples live their lives free of conflict while others are faced with struggles. Instead, all couples encounter stressful events and they need to possess the tools that help them negotiate and resolve the ever changing demands of life. Again, these tools include maintaining a level of motivation for approaching life and its challenges, establishing a meaningful way for comprehending the relationship and life's challenges such that understanding and meaning lead to constructive behavior and, finally, maintaining an ability to manage behavior within the relationship so that suitable planning occurs and so that life's problems get resolved. Consequently, we think it is important for counselors to appreciate these tools in order to develop therapeutic interventions that can impact the couple's relationship.

Motivation

Obviously, a couple need to remain motivated to pursue their relationship, to resolve life's tasks, and to search out new tasks that pose a challenge and opportunity for growth. This motivation is based on an interest in maintaining the relationship and an optimistic sense that the relationship can not only weather storms but also be strengthened in the process. There are, of course, numerous indicators of low motivation and some include a limited willingness to respond to one's partner's needs as well as limited investment in verbalizing one's own desires, a reduced effort in spending time together or in establishing rituals for the relationship, and a limited amount of time spent in planning for the future of the relationship. On the other hand, higher levels of motivation for maintaining the relationship are exemplified as partners share and respond to each other's concerns, make time for their relationship, and plan for the future. Motivation for developing the relationship is related to the reciprocal behaviors demonstrated between partners and, so, the level of motivation is often associated with patterns of interaction that manifest themselves as the couple solve problems and work their way through life's transitions.

Meaning

The couple's comprehension or their way of understanding how they relate to each other is also important to their ability to pursue their relationship in a way that allows life's tasks to get negotiated and that provides for new opportunities for continued growth. Here, it becomes important for the partners to see the reciprocal nature of their relationship and to realize that they both help to define the ills as well as the strengths of the relationship. Put more simply, they become aware that 'By changing myself, I can change the relationship.' This is quite different from the view that describes the behavior of partners as not reciprocal or that suggests the behavior of one is not influenced and does not impact on the other. This view indicates that any individual can only influence her or his own behavior and, so, we often hear partners describing their mates as thoughtful, lazy, strong, weak, etc. as if their partner's behavior was in no way influenced by anyone outside of themselves. Minuchin and Fishman (1981) have made a similar point by way of commenting on complementarity in family relationships. It would seem that when couples comprehend their relationship as being more interactional in nature, and realize that 'we do influence each other,' more opportunity for growth can be realized. As a consequence, it would also seem that a reciprocal or interactive view of the relationship would increase the couple's motivation to pursue the relationship.

Management

The couple's ability to manage their behavior relates to their ability to communicate in ways that allow them to be heard by one another as well as their ability to organize their relationship so that tasks get accomplished. It is often during periods of high stress, when conditions within the relationship require some change, that we most clearly notice problems in communicating and in organizing the relationship. For example, it can occur that a couple's pattern of communication includes one partner dominating the talk time and the other assuming the role of a listener, or that both are locked in an escalating conflict, or that both are withdrawing from each other and, consequently, there is a deficit of communication. These patterns of communication reflect how the couple organize their relationship; for instance, when only one talks for the couple we might notice decision making being placed in the hands of one partner, when both are locked in escalating conflict we might notice each decision becoming a struggle for power and control, and when there is a deficit of communication we might notice the couple in a disengaged relationship and observe that decision making suffers. On the other hand, when a couple can discuss conditions that impact on their relationship in such a way that each feels heard and understood, then each partner is often more open to accommodating to the requirements of the life events facing them. Under these conditions counselors are more likely to observe flexibility, where partners organize their relationship so that they share the leadership position depending on the demands of the situation. For instance, if one partner is experiencing increased demands at work the other can become more involved at home or, if the birth of a second child requires additional domestic commitments, then the couple might reorganize their relationship so that both become more involved in parenting. It is not that there is one right way for couples to communicate and organize their relationship, but couples who retain flexibility in organizing their relationship are more likely to resolve life's tasks in a way that brings greater satisfaction to the relationship.

The management of marriages is more often an issue of motivation than one of behavioral skills. Unhappily married couples usually have the skills to communicate effectively, but for many reasons they choose not to use those skills in their relationship. Thus, Gottman (1979) has said that unhappily married couples suffer from a 'performance' rather than a 'skills' deficit. One might ask, why then is management an area of intervention? There are three basic reasons: (a) sometimes, although rarely, couples actually lack the management skills necessary to negotiate their marriage; (b) sometimes couples, by discussing and practicing communication and management skills under the direction of a counselor, clarify the priorities of their relationship and become more motivated to change; and (c) sometimes practicing management skills allows couples a way of 'saving face', of showing a renewed interest in their relationship by learning skills, even if they already possess them without having to confess that they had previously been very unmotivated to improve their relationship. Thus, behavioral management becomes the third component of our three-part model for understanding effective functioning in an intimate relationship. Counseling interventions for increasing a couple's level of motivation, for expanding the comprehension or meaning they attribute to their relationship, and for challenging their patterns of interaction will be discussed in Chapters 4, 5, 6 and 7.

Summary

With this introductory chapter to couples counseling, we have attempted to introduce our thoughts on the nature of couple relationships, we have presented areas commonly offered by clients as problematic in their relationship, and we have described three tools or abilities that can help couples in resolving concerns. It is also our hope that an explanation of the chapters to follow will provide the reader with an orientation to this text.

Chapter 2 is rather theoretical in nature and discusses systemic variables that counselors will want to consider in helping to bring about a change in the couple's relationship. Chapter 3 provides the reader with an outline of how to handle the initial couples counseling session as well as thought on how to organize follow-up sessions. Chapter 4 focuses on interventions designed to increase the couple's motivation for working together toward change. Couples often view their relationship as comprised of two separate and conflicting personalities. Chapter 5, however, concentrates on a discussion of counselor interventions designed to help the couple appreciate the interactional nature of their relationship, and how each is not only influenced by the other but also impacts on the other.

Chapter 6 offers a discussion of in-session interventions for destabilizing the couple's accustomed and nonproductive patterns of interaction. Managing out-of-session behavior is the focus of Chapter 7, and we have discussed using homework assignments to challenge the interactional sequences that have kept the couple stuck in an unsatisfactory relationship. Finally, Chapter 8 offers a discussion of special issues commonly encountered by counselors involved in couples counseling. We hope that, in studying this book, the reader doesn't indiscriminately try to use the ideas or interventions mentioned. Rather, we would hope that readers would be stimulated to consider the range of nonproductive patterns that couples can engage in and then generate interventions that particularly suit the couples in their own practices.

experience, believe that more positive outcomes occur when couples are seen jointly. There is an intrinsic logic to the perspective that if there is a problem in a relationship it would be more helpful to see all of the parties involved rather than seeing just one. A commitment to seeing couples jointly may also be gained from reviewing the empirical research related to couples counseling outcomes.

In one of the more extensive reviews of research on marital counseling outcomes, Gurman, Kniskern, and Pinsof (1986) discussed general findings relative to marital counseling and more specific findings when the dyad is involved in the treatment of specific clinical disorders. Without belaboring the research studies they present, we will review some of their basic conclusions relative to marital counseling. The reader is urged to study their work and that of the researchers they reviewed to gain a clearer understanding of the variables studied and the research designs. The main findings include:

- Marital counseling, in general, leads to positive outcomes and the effects of treatment are more positive than receiving no treatment.
- There is a greater chance of success in marital counseling when the spouses are seen conjointly in treatment.
- Positive results in marital counseling usually occur in short-term treatment, less than 20 sessions.
- As in any counseling, marital counseling may be associated with both couple and individual deterioration.
- A 'style' of stimulating interaction and giving support in early treatment sessions tends to encourage couple stability, whereas providing little structure and confrontation of highly affective material tends to lead to deterioration.
- A number of studies report positive clinical outcomes for affective and anxiety disorders, as well as an increase in marital satisfaction, when the dyad is involved in the therapeutic process but the focus of treatment is the index client's symptoms.

While a summary of these research findings suggests some optimism about the efficacy of couples counseling, it is important to keep in mind that the research in this area can have inherent problems. For instance, efforts to standardize treatment procedures, in order that research designs can be replicated and findings generalized to practitioners, are indeed problematic. Counselors' idiosyncratic styles and their levels of experience make the standardization of treatment difficult if not impossible and, as

2

Domains of Intervention and System Variables Targeted for Change

In some ways the job of a couples counselor can be likened to t
of a travel tour guide. Guides use their knowledge of the territo
to be explored and of the groups they are responsible for to ma
decisions and recommendations about what sites are worth seei
and what should be avoided. They determine the sequence in whic
a group will view the attractions and they make accommodation
and try to create an atmosphere that will optimize the group'
enjoyment and learning.

Likewise, counselors use their knowledge of couple and family
relationships as well as the therapeutic change process to attempt
to help couples focus on aspects of their relationship that offer
hope and satisfaction. The counselor also attempts to draw the
couple's attention away from aspects of their relationship that are
not satisfying or that offer them little in terms of making their relationship better.

In this process, counselors depend on knowledge gained from
research to provide them with important information about the
impact of counseling on couples. Counselors also depend on thei
own experience and the experience of others to help them under
stand the organizing principles of couple relationships as well a
the structures in these relationships that are amenable to change
In this chapter we will first briefly review some research finding
relative to couples counseling. Then, we will discuss majo
constructs used to understand a couple's relationship. The
constructs describe the aspects of a couple's relationship that a
targeted for intervention and change.

Impact of Couples Counseling

Couples counseling assumes that there are more positive outcom
for certain kinds of problems and conditions by seeing the cou
as a dyad rather than by seeing them individually. Such a view m
emanate from the clinical judgment of those who have seen coup
both jointly and individually and, as a result of their clini

Todd and Stanton (1983) suggested, developing a standardized treatment manual may in fact be in conflict with the principle of counselor flexibility. Moreover, when discussing the use of parallel treatments for comparing the effect of procedures, Todd and Stanton noted, 'It seems virtually impossible to have one therapist conduct two different treatments with equal expectations about the effectiveness of the treatments and equal skill in conducting them' (1983: 102). They also discussed the difficulty in developing a control group for couples counseling research and mentioned the ethical problem of establishing a control group from a waiting-list.

Furthermore, research on couples counseling must address the nature of the dependent variable to be studied; that is, 'What change is desired as a result of counseling?' Here, there needs to be some parallel between the theoretical model of treatment and the desired change. For instance, a behavioral approach to counseling might measure change through an increase or decrease in targeted behavior of one or both members of the relationship. A systems model, however, would consider not only change in the targeted member of the relationship but also changes within the relationship, such as the wife's reduced depression and the couple's ability to share more in decision making. In order to more adequately assess change in the couple's subsystem, it may be necessary to collect information on the couple's relationship as well as from individual members in the relationship.

Although conducting research on couples counseling may not be a high priority for many practitioners, evaluating the effectiveness of one's practice is often desirable. The evaluation of counseling effectiveness is tied closely to assessment and goal setting and we will mention these two topics in Chapter 3. We will now discuss those constructs defined by theoreticians and practitioners as important in bringing about change with couples.

Couple Variables Targeted for Change

Don and Barbara have been married for 25 years. In the counselor's office they express concern over Barbara's depression, which they describe as low grade but chronic during the past few years. Barbara describes her depression as having worsened in the past few months and associates this in time with the marriage of their youngest daughter. This daughter married six months ago and moved to a distant city. The oldest daughter left home some time ago and now is only able to visit her family once a year, at Christmas. The couple have become quite successful in their community with Don putting long hours into the family business. Historically, Barbara devoted herself to parenting and helped Don at the family store but, with the success of the business, three years ago Don insisted that she stop working and enjoy herself at home.

This brief case illustration suggests that Don and Barbara's marriage can be effectively understood as a social system. Constructs used for understanding the couple as a social system include: (a) the couple as a subsystem of the family; (b) the couple's adjustment to stages of life cycle development; (c) the rules and boundaries that govern interaction within the couple's relationship; and (d) the level of homeostasis within the couple's relationship. We will now describe these systems variables and relate them to couples counseling.

The Couple as a Subsystem of the Family

A system can be thought of as any unit with a series of interacting parts. For example, Goldenberg and Goldenberg mentioned that in a family system 'Each member of the family influences and is influenced by the other members; over time, their transactions become patterns that shape the behavior of all participants within the system' (1980: 30). This also holds for the couple's relationship; each partner influences and is influenced by the other partner. Moreover, every system is comprised of interacting subsystems and family members are influenced by the interactive behaviors of individuals in different subsystems. These subsystems can be formed along gender or generation lines as well as with regard to functional requirements and interests (Minuchin, 1974). For instance, Minuchin noted that a family system may consist of a spousal subsystem, a parental subsystem, and a sibling subsystem, and a couple may find themselves belonging to the spousal and parental subsystems and, perhaps, to a sibling subsystem from their families of origin.

The spousal subsystem is seen as basic to the development of the family: 'it is central to the life of the family in its early years, and continues to play a major role over the life span of the family. There is little doubt that the overall success of the family is to a large extent dependent upon the ability of the husband and wife to work out a successful relationship with one another' (Goldenberg & Goldenberg, 1990: 45). In addition, Minuchin (1974) mentioned that the spousal subsystem provides partners with a refuge from external stress while also fostering opportunities for creativity and growth. On the other hand, he suggested that the couple's subsystem may also open opportunities for conflict through efforts

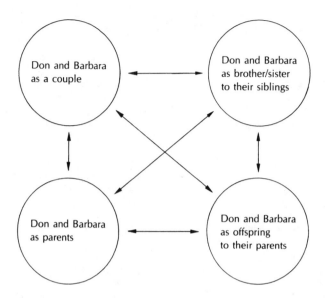

Figure 2.1 *Interacting subsystems*

to improve or change one's partner. We suggest that counselors need to acknowledge the existence of the couple's subsystem and need to realize that the subsystem is more than simply two individuals in a relationship. That is, the reader will hopefully gain an appreciation for how individuals in a relationship can be shaped or influenced by patterns of interaction in the couple's subsystem as well as the larger family system.

In this chapter's case illustration (see Figure 2.1) we would not be surprised to discover that Don and Barbara had become so busy with the family business and parenting that they lost sight of the importance of their relationship. That is, with so much time and energy being devoted to the family business and the children, little was left for nurturing the couple's subsystem. As a result, when the last daughter moved out of the home and Barbara 'retired' from work, Don and Barbara found themselves in a situation where little was felt between them to keep their relationship alive. As a matter of fact, if it weren't for Barbara's depression, there may have been nothing for them to discuss or share.

Stages of Couple Development
The family system and the marital subsystem can also be viewed as units moving through time. As the couple's relationship develops,

Years in the relationship	Sample tasks
Early years	Becoming independent of parents
Second to fourth years	Having children, establishing traditions as well as values
Third to seventh years	Balancing commitments to marriage, children and careers
Seventh to fifteenth years	Evaluating how well commitments to marriage, childrearing, career, and broader community have been maintained
Fifteenth to twenty-fourth years	Separating from parenting involvement
Twenty-fourth to thirty-fifth years	Children leaving home, death of one's own parents, questioning traditionally assigned roles
After thirty-fifth years	More freedom from some responsibilities and new issues like illness and loss of a partner

Figure 2.2   *Couple's life cycle*

it encounters different tasks in the life cycle that require an adjustment of the subsystem. Monte (1989) noted that individual and couple changes through the life cycle are related; that is, a change in one ensures change in the other. His model relates to heterosexual middle class couples who are of about the same age and he describes developmental tasks facing couples as they move through the life cycle. Whatever developmental model counselors use in working with couples, establishing an understanding of the issues faced at different stages in the life cycle will help illuminate an appreciation of needed changes in the relationship.

Monte's (1989) model (see Figure 2.2) can be used in understanding relationship development through the life cycle. For instance, a couple in their mid-20s, who are in the first years of their marriage, might experience a struggle in becoming independent of their parents while also attempting to effectively communicate needs to one another. In the second to fourth years of the relationship the 'honeymoon' starts to fade and the couple become involved with having children and developing careers, and in establishing their own traditions and values. During the third to seventh years, Monte mentioned the couple are faced with a continuation or need to increase commitment in a number of areas: for instance, commitment to the marriage, children and their life's work. Here, tension can be noticed as the couple attempt to balance commitments in these three areas. By the seventh to the fifteenth years of the relationship, patterns of decision making, conflict resolution, and accomplishing tasks have become well established. The relationship can now be evaluated according to how well it has maintained commitments to the relationship, child-rearing, life's work and the broader community.

By the fifteenth to twenty-fourth years of the relationship, the partners are now in their early 40s and looking back and evaluating their lives as individuals and as a couple. Their children are now teenagers, the couple are separating from involvement in parenting, and they are again struggling to define their identity. During the twenty-fifth to thirty-fifth years of the relationship, the partners are in their 50s and early 60s. The children are leaving home, the couple may be coping with the death of their parents, and perhaps questioning traditionally assigned roles: for example, the roles of homemaker and bread winner. Hopefully, after thirty-five years the relationship has become a source of intimacy, nurturance and personal growth. With more freedom from responsibilities (children and work), this can become a phase of vitality in the couple's relationship. Obviously, it is also a period of change as the couple face new issues like illness or the impending loss of a partner.

Of course, movement through these phases proceeds at an idio-syncratic pace. When spouses are of differing ages, have children later in life or experience a blended family their developmental course may differ from that just described. It does appear, however, that the couple's relationship is not a static one but one that changes and develops as the couple are faced with new issues at different points in the life cycle.

Haley (1973) suggested that if the family system, and we would include the couple's subsystem, has difficulty accomplishing its developmental tasks, one member of the family may develop problems in living that bring them to a counselor's office. The effect that these problems have is to divert the couple's attention from their impasse at resolving a developmental task and to refocus their attention onto one member of the family or couple. For the counselor who views the couple from other than a systemic perspective, it is especially easy to focus on one partner rather than the relationship. In our case illustration, a systemic model would conceptualize Don and Barbara as struggling with the launching stage of the life cycle where the children are leaving home. The youngest daughter has married and moved to a distant city. Barbara no longer works in the family business and, with Don putting extra hours into the family business, it may be that the only way Don and Barbara come together as a couple is around Barbara's illness.

Rules and Boundaries Governing Couple Relationships

Family rules are nonverbally-agreed-to behaviors that are outside the family members' awareness (Dodson & Kurpius, 1977), and rules are set up to govern behaviors in the couple's subsystem as well as the larger family system. These rules seem to develop slowly over time as the couple negotiate their relationship, and the rules can be observed in patterns of interaction the couple demonstrate as they go about living their life together. More specifically, the rules reflect how the couple spend their time, what they talk about, who they spend time with, and whether they have a dominant–submissive or competitive relationship. Lederer and Jackson's (1968) notion about a dominant–submissive relationship (complementary style) and a competitive relationship (symmetrical style) can be understood from the perspective of rules that govern the power and influence issues in the relationship (see Figure 2.3).

Complementary relationship   One partner is 'in charge' of the relationship while the other becomes the 'follower' e.g. one is seen as competent and the other as incompetent or one as parental and the other as childlike.

Symmetrical relationship   Both partners compete to demonstrate their power and influence e.g. they may quarrel to get in the last word or to prove the other wrong.

Figure 2.3   *Dyadic relationships*

For instance, in every relationship responsibility exists for initiating and carrying out certain tasks. With partners in a marriage, these tasks are almost infinite in number: handling finances and relationships with extended family, responding to social and civic requests, initiating and participating in intimacy and sexual practices, pursuing and accelerating career opportunities, etc. When the couple develop rules for their relationship that suggest they share the leader and follower roles, one partner can take responsibility for some tasks while the other becomes the follower and around other tasks these roles can be reversed. When the couple feel confident enough to share leader and follower roles, they retain flexibility in responding to life's tasks. On the other hand, when the rules suggest that one person is always in charge and the other is always the follower, the couple are at risk of experiencing difficulty in resolving tasks and they may decompensate into a situation where one partner experiences some sort of distress. When rules for the relationship suggest that both partners need to exert their power and influence, conflict often results and, again, family tasks don't get resolved. In working with couples, counselors will want to be aware of rules that govern the relationship and that manifest themselves in repeated patterns of behavior.

Rules that govern the couple's relationship can also be seen in boundaries (Minuchin, 1974) that exist between the couple around various issues (handling their sexual relationship and opportunities for intimacy) and between the couple and those outside their relationship (establishing commitments to one's career and friends). Boundaries exist on a continuum from rigid to diffuse (see Figure 2.4). Rigid boundaries indicate little involvement between partners and little involvement between the couple and those outside the couple's subsystem. More diffuse boundaries suggest overinvolvement between the partners in each other's lives and overinvolvement between the couple and those outside the couple's subsystem. Between the rigid and diffuse boundaries exists a clear area where the couple interact with each other without losing their individuality and they interact with others outside the couple's subsystem but not at the price of neglecting their relationship.

Rigid boundaries The partners demonstrate little involvement with each other (e.g. more like distant acquaintances than intimate partners) and/or little involvement with others outside their relationship (e.g. limited friendships and contact with extended family).

Diffuse boundaries Partners are overinvolved in each other's lives (e.g. likely to speak for each other and be so involved with one another that there's no life separate from the relationship) and/or overinvolved in activities outside the relationship (e.g. so involved in life outside the relationship that there's little left for oneself or one's partner).

Figure 2.4 *Rigid and diffuse boundaries*

Whether rules in the couple's relationship suggest a diffuse or rigid boundary or a complementary or symmetrical style, the rules are demonstrated through repetitive patterns of behavior that show up as the couple attempt to resolve problems in the life cycle. Rules or patterns of behavior are often most clear when the couple are unsuccessfully trying to resolve or cope with some life cycle task that is, a stressor that is internal to the family. In addition, Minuchin (1974) has identified three other types of stressful events encountered by couples: a stressor experienced by one member but external to the family, such as one partner receiving a job promotion; a stressor experienced by the entire family and also external to the family, such as moving to a new community; and/or a stressor that is idiosyncratic to the family, such as living with a chronically ill member. The point is that no couple exists stress free and the couple's rules or patterns of behavior are viewed as influential in determining how well the couple negotiate stressful events and their subsequent life adjustment.

In our case illustration of Don and Barbara, rules in the couple's subsystem might have suggested that men are to be workaholics, women are to be spared from working outside the home, women have responsibility for home life and the husband is to be the decision maker in the marriage. These rules would provide for a dominant–submissive relationship, with a rather rigid boundary between Don and Barbara, at a time in the life cycle when they were trying to cope with the launching of their children. Here, Barbara's depression may become the primary vehicle for bringing the couple together as they try to fill the void left by the departure of their youngest daughter.

Homeostasis within the Couple Relationship

As previously mentioned, the couple relationship can be viewed as a subsystem of a larger social system that is, in part, governed by nonverbally-agreed-to rules as it passes through various stages of development. The couple must show some ability to change their rules for relating to each other as the relationship matures while also holding on to some rules in order to maintain a level of stability in the relationship. This tendency to try to maintain a steady or stable state of equilibrium is referred to as homeostasis (Goldenberg & Goldenberg, 1990). Goldenberg and Goldenberg commented on cybernetic theory as described by Norbert Wiener (1967). They suggested how change and homeostasis in the relationship are governed by negative and positive feedback loops (see Figure 2.5).

Within the couple's subsystem, negative feedback is corrective and indicates to the couple that too much change is being called for and that they need to return to previously used rules or patterns of interaction. Positive feedback within the relationship indicates that change is acceptable and that new rules or patterns of interaction can be entertained. For example, when one party suggests that she

Negative feedback in the relationship suggests that too much challenging or changing of family rules has occurred and the couple need to return to using previously accepted rules of interaction.

Positive feedback in the relationship suggests that new rules of interacting can be entertained and perhaps accepted.

Figure 2.5 *Negative and positive feedback*

may take a promotion that would require more time away from the relationship, her partner might continue to read the newspaper or even get up to find the sports page (negative feedback), or he might put down the paper and nonverbally as well as verbally indicate a receptiveness to a new arrangement in their relationship (positive feedback). Moreover, Nichols (1984) suggested that, in a couple's relationship, the disturbed behavior of one member may actually function as a unit of negative feedback. For instance, when rules for managing the relationship do not change to meet the needs of the changing life cycle and its accompanying tasks, it is not unusual to find the submissive member in a complementary relationship becoming an identified patient or the partners in a symmetrical relationship becoming embroiled in conflict. The couple then focus attention on problems of the identified patient or the righteousness of individual and conflictual perspectives rather than looking at the appropriateness of the rules for governing the relationship. While we do not see this as a preplanned diversion, it does distract the couple from looking at how they are managing their relationship.

Homeostasis can also be maintained and needed changes in the relationship ignored by triangling a third person, object, or illness into the relationship. Triangling is a family systems construct introduced by Murray Bowen. Bowen (1978) noted that two-person systems are not stable and, when stress occurs between members of a dyad, a triad may be formed. For example, when life cycle demands or other environmental stressors produce tension in the relationship, rather than discuss needed changes in the their own subsystem, the couple can focus their concern on a person (child or in-law), object (bills), or illness (depression). In a similar manner to the previous paragraph, we are not suggesting that triangling is a preplanned diversion, but it does distract the couple from looking at how they are managing their relationship.

Triangling (see Figure 2.6) may show up as a protective concern for or critical demand of a third person. Minuchin (1974) referred

---

Detouring Couple conflict is diverted by a demonstrated pattern of protective concern for another (e.g. the couple worrying or being concerned for children) or criticism of another individual (e.g. the couple censuring children for their behavior).

Cross-generational coalition The couple are in conflict and one partner forms a coalition with a child against the other partner (e.g. mother and daughter find fault with father).

Figure 2.6 *Triangling patterns*

to this as detouring and suggested that concern for or demands of a third person may actually be replacing or masking conflict in the couple's relationship. Another type of triangle takes the form of a cross-generational coalition (Haley, 1976). Here, Haley suggested that when the couple are in conflict one partner and child form a connection against the other partner. For example, a coalition may form around a father and son feeling that the mother is too demanding and critical. Or, a coalition may form around mother and son feeling that the father is neglectful or irresponsible toward the family. Not only does parenting become difficult in these situations, but it is also likely that, with the son being triangled into the couple's relationship, spousal issues (wife's criticalness and husband's peripheral position) will go unresolved. The central idea here is that by triangling in a third person, object, or illness, customary and homeostatic patterns of behavior are maintained and rules that govern the relationship go unchanged.

In our case illustration, Don and Barbara's family is in the phase of life where children are being launched from the family and the couple have established some degree of financial security for themselves, yet they hold on to outdated rules for the relationship. That is, Don continues to put unnecessarily long hours into the business and it appears Barbara continues to see herself as assigned to the home while Don makes the decisions for the couple. By concentrating on Barbara's illness, the couple do not consider possible changes in their relationship. For example, Barbara is not faced with finding satisfaction outside the home nor is Don faced with finding enjoyment outside his work.

Summary

Hopefully, viewing the couple as a subsystem of a larger family, comprehending stages of relationship development, obtaining an appreciation of the impact of rules and boundaries on the relationship, and grasping how homeostasis can be maintained will help counselors view couples' relationships as being more complex than the sum of two individual and separate personalities. Indeed, these constructs can indicate the difficulty in treating one member of a relationship without understanding the systemic context in which the relationship exists. Returning to our case illustration, a counselor could see Barbara alone and work for years with her in individual counseling. As a matter of fact, by sharing the important and meaningful concerns of her life with a counselor, she may become more intimate with the counselor than she is with her husband. In Chapters 4, 5, 6, and 7 we will focus on procedures counselors can use for working with couples who are stuck in nonproductive and problematic relationships. These procedures include fostering hope in the relationship, generating a new understanding of the relationship based on systemic principles, and managing behavior in the counseling session so that the couple do not recycle old and problematic patterns of interaction. We will now turn the reader from this theoretical understanding of relationships toward a more practical understanding of how to apply these concepts in initial and subsequent counseling sessions.

3

Structuring of the Counselling Session

This chapter provides a brief outline of how counselors can handle the initial telephone contact for couples counseling, the initial couples counseling sessions and the follow-up counseling sessions. The first telephone contact with one of the two partners can be used to collect some quick and basic information: names and addresses and telephone numbers, a short description of the presenting problem and whether both partners will attend the counseling sessions, and who has referred the couple. Finding out early who has referred the couple will, when appropriate, allow the counselor to prepare a release of information form that can be signed by the couple at the first appointment. During the initial phone conversation, the counselor will generally want to avoid trying to create therapeutic change but some general information can be offered: the counselor can mention that it is preferable to see the couple together rather than only one partner, as well as outlining the fee schedule, indicating that the first couple of sessions will be spent getting to know the couple and their concerns, and mentioning that the couple will be asked to commit to a specified duration for counseling. The couple may be told that at the end of the specified period, say eight to twelve weeks, an evaluation will occur to decide whether to continue further counseling or to terminate. The next two sections of this chapter will discuss how the counselor can handle the initial appointments, assessing the couple's relationship and assessing interactions with the extended family as well as the individual functioning of each partner.

Assessing the Couple's Relationship

Haley (1987) suggested five stages in conducting an initial family counseling session: the social stage, the problem stage, the interaction stage, the stage for defining desired changes, and the stage involved with ending the interview. We follow a similar model when conducting an initial couple counseling session and try to develop a therapeutic relationship through utilizing joining procedures: 'Joining is letting the family [couple] know that the therapist understands them and is working with and for them. Only under his protection can the family [couple] have the security to explore alternatives, try the unusual, and change. Joining is the glue that holds the therapeutic system together' (Minuchin & Fishman, 1981: 31–2).

Minuchin and Fishman suggested that joining with the couple can occur from a close, median, or disengaged position. From a close position the counselor can reflect and recognize positive qualities of the relationship as well as difficulties and pain experienced by the couple, 'Your willingness to stay together through these difficult times seems to indicate a real commitment to the marriage' or 'You both feel angry and neglected by the other.' From a median position the counselor may track the content of each partner's remarks, 'Tell me more about that . . . and then what happened?' Also from a median position the counselor can honor the process in the couple's relationship by showing respect for preferred patterns of interaction; for instance, interacting at first with the more dominant partner in a complementary relationship or by acknowledging the importance of differing perspectives in a symmetrical relationship. Later, of course, the counselor might want to challenge these relationship dynamics. From the disengaged position, joining can occur by creating a sense of hope in the couple that the counselor is competent to work with their relationship. For instance, by providing a direction for the session or by supporting some behaviors and challenging others the counselor sends the message that she or he is prepared to provide the counseling session with a direction. Efforts at joining are important to the initial appointment and they need to occur throughout couples counseling, particularly at those points where the counselor becomes alienated from the couple. What follows utilizes many thoughts from Strategic Family Therapy (Haley, 1987), Structural Family Therapy (Minuchin, 1974; Minuchin & Fishman, 1981), and Brief Therapy (de Shazer, 1985, 1988).

Social Stage

The social stage is an opportunity to introduce oneself, to find out by which name each partner wants to be called, to find out who lives at home, to find out more about what each partner does in terms of a career and what they do for recreation, and to find out how long the couple have been together. Haley (1987) suggested that, by engaging each partner in this 'light' manner, the counselor is sending the message that each is to be involved in counseling. Here, the counselor can also work at joining with each partner by disclosing a little about herself or himself (say, being the parent of teenagers or enjoying similar recreational activities) or by simply tracking, following, and pursuing the content of each partner's remarks (Minuchin, 1974). If one partner wants to start discussing the presenting problem, Haley (1987) suggested that the counselor might be best advised to observe how the other responds and then to tell each partner that the counselor is interested in what they have to say but first would like to get to know a little about each of them as individuals.

Problem Stage
During this stage each partner is asked to clearly describe the problem as they see it. Haley (1987) suggested that the counselor might start by briefly sharing what she or he already knows about the presenting problem from the initial telephone call and, then, ask each partner to tell the counselor what they see as the presenting problem. Here, the counselor wants to get a clear picture of the presenting problem so each partner is encouraged, one at a time, to talk to the counselor and, as Haley suggested, they are discouraged from talking with one another about their concern. We find it most helpful when we can talk with couples in specific, usually behavioral, ways about their problems. For instance, the counselor wants to know about the date of onset and concurrent events as well as the frequency of the problem, and which events currently trigger the problem and how both partners are responding to the problem. The counselor is trying to establish a clear and behaviorally specific description of the presenting problem. If, for example, the couple say 'We just don't get along' the counselor responds with 'What's an example of this?' or when one says about a partner 'He's too impatient' the counselor responds with 'What does he do that signals his impatience?' We also want to ascertain what is going on when the problem is not present. With regard to this, we might ask, 'What are you doing when you do get along?' or 'Tell me about a time when he has been patient.' By these latter two efforts we are trying to instill hope by identifying successful exceptions (de Shazer, 1988) and to ascertain the couple's level of motivation by seeing whether positive moments in their relationship are possible.

Tracking (Minuchin, 1974) is also helpful in facilitating joining and in obtaining a clearer description of the presenting problem. For example, after one spouse describes the other's impatience as criticisms delivered when chores have been forgotten, the counselor tracks by asking 'And what do you do in response to his comment?' and 'How do you respond to her reactions?' and, eventually, 'How does this interaction end?' Such tracking provides the counselor with a limited slice of the couple's pattern of interaction. After a period of tracking, it is occasionally easy to offer an empathic statement that can also facilitate joining from a close position such as 'I certainly hear your hope that the relationship can improve.'

During this stage it is best not to share one's impressions about the relationship but merely to catalog them in one's memory bank (Haley, 1987). Also, it is not the time to provide advice, even if the couple request it. Instead, the counselor can simply let them know that she or he would first like to gather more information (Haley, 1987). Similarly, the counselor does not want either partner to talk too long on their view of the problem (Haley, 1987). If one partner monopolizes the time, the other might start to believe that her or his mate is establishing an alliance with the counselor from which she or he is excluded. Generally, each partner would receive about five minutes to share perceptions of the couple's complaint(s).

Interaction Stage

After receiving a clear or specific description of the couple's presenting problem, the counselor directs the couple to interact with each other. Minuchin and Fishman (1981) have referred to this as creating an enactment. The point is to have the couple demonstrate how they deal with or handle their problems. For instance, if one partner is depressed, the counselor might direct that person to pretend to be depressed and the other to demonstrate how she or he tries to be helpful. Or, if a couple complain about escalating conflict in their relationship, the counselor might ask them to discuss and try to resolve some volatile issue. As the couple are interacting, the counselor is watching for redundant behavioral and emotional patterns as well as listening for a possible third person, activity, or illness that has been triangled into the relationship. Because each partner is part of the relationship and contributes to these patterns, neither is usually able to describe them accurately and, as a result, the counselor creates an opportunity to observe the patterns during the interaction stage. It is at this time that the counselor may want to test the couple's level of homeostasis or openness to change by suggesting an alternative to the accustomed pattern of interaction. For instance, during an attack and counterattack sequence the counselor might direct each partner to state to the other what they are willing to do to bring about change or, during a pattern where one is dominant and the other is submissive, the submissive partner might be asked to describe desired changes in the relationship. In part, these directives are given to see whether the couple's relationship is flexible enough to accommodate new patterns of interacting, and the counselor's directive stance may help in joining from an expert and disengaged position (Minuchin & Fishman, 1981).

Defining Desired Changes and Ending the Interview

The last stage of the initial couple's interview combines the last two stages of Haley's (1987) initial family interview. Here the counselor is checking in with each partner to see if there is agreement on the goals of counseling. Haley suggested that the goals of counseling need to relate to solvable issues and we would suggest that for couples counseling they can include (a) reducing some problem behavior, such as conflict, commitments outside the relationship, procrastination or forgetfulness and, possibly, (b) beginning or increasing some desired behavior, such as spending time together, fulfilling chores or creating opportunities for pursuing individual interests. The counselor will want to inform the couple again of the closed-ended time period for counseling. With the closed time period, the counselor is attempting to send a message that counseling does not go on for ever, and we have found it more productive if everyone knows that at a set time the amount of movement in couples counseling will be evaluated. It is important at this point for the couple to know that the second session will also be devoted to collecting more information from them with regard to their relationship with extended family members and with regard to themselves as individuals.

Finally, as Haley (1987) suggested, the counselor may want to assign some type of homework to challenge the couple's pattern of interaction. This homework is usually for the purpose of evaluating the couple's openness to change. If they return to the following session having completed the homework, they are suggesting that there is some receptivity to change. If homework has not been completed, however, it suggests that the couple's relationship may be maintained by a higher level of homeostasis and is more reluctant to change. The counselor may also find that she or he needs the time between sessions to better understand the couple's problematic patterns of interaction and to develop homework for challenging these patterns. As a result, the session can end with the counselor simply scheduling the next appointment and mentioning,

> Between now and next time we meet, we [I] would like you to observe, so that you can describe to us [me] next time, what happens in your [pick one: family, life, marriage, relationship] that you want to continue to have happen. (de Shazer, 1985: 137)

As de Shazer noted, with this directive clients begin to look for worthwhile aspects of their relationship, which, in itself, is a change from focusing on their dissatisfaction, and he mentions that some clients have reported changes in the interval between the first and second sessions.

Assessing Interactions with the Extended Family as well as Levels of Individual Functioning

When the couple arrive for the second session the counselor engages in a brief period of social interchange with each partner and then lets them know that she or he would like to collect some further information with regard to their relationship and with regard to them as individuals. The counselor will want to collect this information through completing a genogram (see Chapter 5 for a discussion of genograms). The genogram will include information such as each partner's age, the date of their marriage and whether there have been previous marriages, the number of children in the relationship, and the names and ages of family-of-origin members and whether they are alive or deceased. In order to flesh out the genogram, the counselor will then ask the couple about their current interaction with extended family members, where these family members live, the frequency and type of contact, and whether extended family members are involved with the couple's presenting problem and the nature of their involvement. In addition, each partner is asked about current social relationships to find out about the nature of support from outside the family and to find out if social contacts impact on the couple's presenting problem. The counselor then explores the past family history to find out about early relationships with each set of parents, the nature of the parents' relationship with children, and the nature of sibling relationships. The couple's work and/or academic history is explored to find out if one or both work outside the home and to see if their work or relationships with coworkers contributes to the presenting problem. Thus, this exploration can uncover patterns of interaction in the relationship as well as between the couple and extended family members and significant others.

With regard to levels of individual functioning, both partners are asked about their medical history and whether they have experienced previous counseling. The counselor would like to know if a previous condition could be interacting with current problems in the relationship; this might be early child abuse, current substance abuse, or any medical condition. Of course, during the interview each partner's appearance (clean, unkempt, bizarre), attitude (domineering, provocative, uncooperative), psychomotor activity (accelerated, slowed, inappropriate), and mood (appropriate, anxious, depressed) can be observed. Finally, the counselor also pays attention to each partner's orientation to time, place and person, memory capabilities (immediate, recent, remote), and thought processes (delusions and hallucinations). Disturbances in these areas might be suggestive of psychoses or organic difficulties and would indicate the importance of a psychiatric consultation. Counselors may also decide to use screening inventories to help in assessing the individual's functioning. The Symptom Checklist-90-R (Derogatis, 1977) is one inventory we have employed in screening individual partners for couples counseling. Moreover, with regard to individual evaluations, we have found it helpful for counselors to be familiar with the nosology in the *Diagnostic and Statistical Manual of Mental Disorders* (American Psychiatric Association, 1987). If any of these areas of individual functioning seem atypical, they are explored in more depth and it may be that some presenting problems will require an individual treatment modality (such as counseling or medical) in conjunction with couples counseling.

Once again then, the first couple session is oriented toward assessing perceptions of the presenting problem and patterns of interaction within the relationship and, in the second session, the counselor explores the couple's relationship with extended family members as well as each partner's level of individual functioning. The second session ends with the counselor obtaining an agreement from each partner concerning the objectives of counseling as well as a commitment to a specific number of weeks of counseling. It is agreed that at the end of this time period the counselor and couple will evaluate progress in counseling and decide whether to bring counseling to a close or to negotiate another contract.

An Illustration of the First Two Sessions

Helen called for couples counseling and over the telephone explained that she and her husband Harry had been married for six months and during that time found themselves embroiled in increasing conflict. Helen noted that, while she was calling for the couple, Harry had also expressed his interest in counseling. The counselor noted that the first two sessions would be devoted to learning more about the couple and the history of their relationship. It was mentioned that after the initial sessions the couple and the counselor would attempt to come to a common agreement as to the goals of counseling and then meet for about ten weeks to work towards those common goals. It was also mentioned that at the end of the tenth week the couple and the counselor would decide if the couple had reached their stated objectives and wished to terminate counseling or if they wished to renegotiate their counseling contract. Helen was informed of the counselor's fee schedule and an initial appointment was scheduled.

First Session

Harry and Helen arrived on time for the first session and during the first ten minutes of social interchange Harry noted that Helen had moved to the area about seven months ago. Helen mentioned that she had been a non-tenured faculty member at a university and that she had met Harry two years ago at a conference. Since that time they had maintained a long-distance relationship, getting together on holidays, and moving in with one another when they decided to marry. Harry was a physician and because of his active practice the couple decided to reside in the area where he had established himself. As they began to describe the presenting problem, both mentioned that small disagreements in the past five months had been ignited into major conflicts. For instance, Helen had tried to start a morning ritual of having breakfast together in order to establish some quality time where they could discuss the day's events. While Harry agreed with the importance of quality time, he often found himself so rushed in the mornings that time for breakfast was not available. Helen found herself feeling not appreciated, and the couple slid into conflict as Helen expressed her anger and disappointment and as Harry became defensive. It might also occur that, at the last moment, Harry would suggest they have friends over and Helen would decline, saying she needed more time to prepare for company. Harry would then feel that Helen wasn't being flexible enough and conflict often followed. Both commented that they felt as though their needs were being disregarded.

During the interaction stage of the first session, the counselor asked Harry and Helen to come to a conclusion about how they could spend free time together during the week so that each would find the experience enjoyable. Harry suggested having a couple over from his practice and Helen countered by suggesting dinner and a movie. Each was able to find fault with the other's plan, each defended their own position, and they finally fell into a quiet frustration. Harry then looked to the counselor and said, 'This is where we usually get stuck.' The counselor asked Harry to think of a colleague with whom he had a good relationship and asked Helen to remember a university colleague with whom she worked well. Both were asked to remember how they managed disagreements or conflicts with these colleagues. Harry and Helen were then directed to talk with one another and come up with a way to spend pleasant time together during the week. Harry and Helen settled on a movie and dinner and possibly spending time with Harry's colleagues during the following week.

The counselor brought the first session to a close by suggesting that, not unlike most new couples, Harry and Helen may be struggling with learning to accommodate to one another. It was also noted that this may have been expected since they had been carrying on a long-distance romance during the past year and a half and only recently started living together on a full-time basis. The interview closed with the couple agreeing to schedule a session for the following week.

Second Session

In the second session a genogram was constructed and each partner was asked about current interaction with their extended family (see Figure 3.1). It was noted that both sets of parents were deceased but Harry's ex-wife was alive and had custody of their three-year-old daughter. It was also noted that this daughter spent every other weekend with Harry and Helen. With regard to their social life, Harry mentioned that his practice kept him so busy that he never really developed much of a social life outside his business and Helen, because of recently moving to the area, hadn't developed a social network either. When asked to describe their families of origin, Harry noted that he was the oldest of three children, that his father had been a physician, and that when he was a child it was always expected that he would also become a doctor. His two sisters had been married for a number of years and did not work outside the home. This had been the model that Harry's parents set, where his mother stayed home and raised the children and his father devoted himself to a career. Helen, on the other hand, had been an only child. Her father died when she was young and her mother went to work as a teacher. During her teenage years Helen became quite independent, worked after school, helped to care for the house, and made friends with her mother's colleagues from school. Both Harry and Helen were high achievers in school and, while Harry's life had revolved around preparing to become a doctor, Helen grew up with an independent life style.

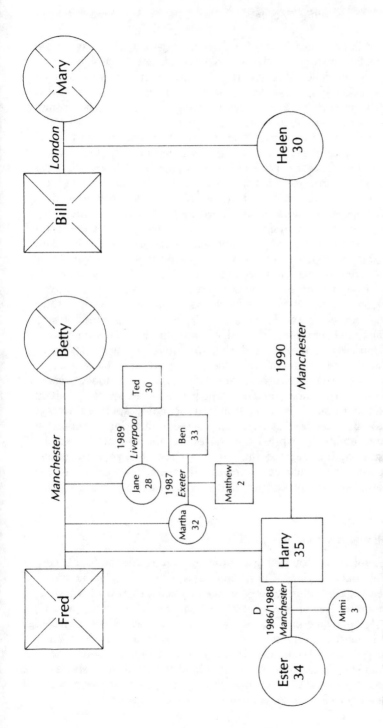

Figure 3.1 *Harry and Helen's genogram (Symbols are explained in Figure 5.2.)*

Neither Harry nor Helen had experienced a significant medical history but Harry noted that part of the problem in his first marriage stemmed from his long hours at work and his wife feeling little support from him, while Helen indicated that her independence had made previous intimate relationships difficult. Although Harry had attempted to use activities like dinner parties to bring the two of them together and Helen tried to establish family rituals for the same purpose, they had not been successful in sharing the leadership role and decision-making process. That is, relative to decision making, the unspoken rule in the relationship was that both needed to assert their dominance so, regardless of the issue, conflict often ensued. From a systemic perspective, this conflict allowed for a homeostatic pattern to continue in the relationship; that is, Harry and Helen were slow to move towards intimacy and able to preserve their independence.

Both Harry and Helen appeared clean and conservatively groomed and dressed. Harry was clean shaven with a short haircut and dressed in suit and tie. Helen had shoulder-length hair and was dressed in skirt and blouse and tweed jacket. Both were cooperative during the interview, answering questions posed to them and, when requested, they elaborated on their remarks. Their psychomotor behavior and mood, orientation and memory, and thought processes all appeared within normal limits. Their intellectual functioning appeared average to above average as suggested by their educational attainment and ability to express themselves. At the end of this second session, both agreed that for ten weeks the goal of couples counseling would be to prevent disagreements from escalating into the type of conflict that each partner later regretted.

Follow-Up Counseling Sessions

The follow-up counseling sessions often resemble the four stages of the initial interview. The session starts with some social interaction, then the counselor focuses on the couple's progress at working on the presenting problem, next the counselor may direct the couple to discuss some part of their relationship in an effort to challenge or support patterns of interaction in the relationship and, finally, the counselor brings the session to a close and, possibly, delivers a homework assignment for the couple. We will now spend some time describing each of these stages as a part of the process of conducting a follow-up couples counseling session.

Social Stage

The social stage allows the counselor and the couple to ease into the counseling session and it also signals to the couple that they are appreciated as people with lives broader than just that of being clients. For instance, it is often easy and enjoyable to start a session by finding out about those things the couple has been involved in during the previous week. If the counselor has had some similar experiences (say, trips or gardening), it allows an opportunity for the counselor to briefly self-disclose and to join with the couple around a common activity (Minuchin, 1974). Again, efforts at joining signal that the counselor understands those unique experiences appreciated by the couple and, as a result, places the counselor in a more influential position when it comes to challenging or supporting the couple's patterns of interaction. The point is that the counselor needs to be able to make human contact rather than simply taking a sterile, objective, clinical stance when interacting with couples.

A Review of the Presenting Problem

When reviewing the presenting problem, the counselor may begin by asking the couple to report on their satisfaction with the previous week. Here the counselor is asking each partner to talk to her or him rather than to their mate. For instance, 'With regard to your presenting problem (say, husband's loss of temper or wife's depression and inability to complete responsibilities), how were things this past week?' Also, if homework was given the counselor wants to follow up and find out if it was completed. As Haley (1987) suggested, if the homework was not completed the counselor may want to express regrets about a missed opportunity. Or, as Haley suggested, the counselor may want to say, 'I'm sorry. I must have misunderstood your desire to resolve this problem.' The counselor might also want to add, 'Perhaps we should go a lot slower in working toward change?' If the homework was completed, however, the counselor does not want to take credit for the improved week but might express surprise that things went so well and attribute the successful week to the couple's investment in the relationship. This is similar to the suggestion offered by Haley with regard to following up on paradoxical directives.

Often, if the couple have had a successful week at resolving their concern, the counselor is wise to find out from each partner what was happening that made the difference, as opposed to focusing on the problem and recycling into a continued discussion of the couple's despair about the relationship. In the next stage of the follow-up session, the interaction stage, partners do not report to the counselor but, instead, they discuss with one another some aspect of the relationship.

Interaction Stage

If during the previous stage the couple reported a continuation of the presenting problem, the counselor might now ask them to bring the presenting problem into the office and, in the here and now, attempt to resolve the problem. For example, if the husband is described as having a difficult time controlling his anger, the couple might be directed to discuss a volatile topic in a manner that would lead to an explosion. The counselor could then assist them in discussing the issue so that the loss of temper might be side-stepped. The counselor might also help them to get their problem-solving efforts back on track after an explosion rather than being derailed by the fracas. Interventions designed to increase the couple's systemic understanding of their relationship (see Chapter 5) and to manage their patterns of interaction (see Chapter 6) might be usefully employed during the interaction stage.

On the other hand, if the week went well for the couple, the counselor may want them to talk with each other about what made things successful as well as how they felt about changes in their pattern of interacting. The couple may be inexperienced at this and their difficulty in responding to the counselor's directive might suggest that there has been a rigid boundary between them when it comes to discussing positive experiences. It may be helpful if the counselor assists the couple in creating a clearer boundary with regard to celebrating positive experiences. For example, the counselor may help the couple continue to talk with each other by having them share and comment on positive feelings from the week, by having them express appreciation of one another, and by having them review hopes for the future. In summary then, the interaction stage during a follow-up session is a period when the couple enact their patterns of interacting and the counselor challenges those which seem to be counterproductive and supports those which seem to lead toward problem resolution.

Bringing the Session to a Close and Assigning
Homework

It seems that a problem with many counseling sessions is that the closing phase is relegated to the last three or four minutes of the session and, if homework is given, the counselor seems surprised at the next appointment to find out that the couple have not followed through with recommendations. Counselors may want to make sure that they allow ten to fifteen minutes for the closing of a session. In fact, after the interaction stage the counselor may want to take a break to consider what type of homework would be most useful in challenging the couple's nonproductive patterns of interaction. In Chapter 7 we discuss developing and delivering homework, but the point here is that homework becomes a vehicle for the counselor to stay involved in the couple's relationship between the sessions and, as a result, it deserves the counselor's consideration. Scheduling a break and stepping out of the counseling room may put just enough emotional distance between the counselor and the couple so that it is easier to reflect on homework that might challenge problematic patterns of interaction as well as support alternative patterns. As Minuchin and Fishman (1981) suggested, the physical distance between a counselor and couple can create a psychological distance that makes it easier to think about systemic dynamics. After returning from the break, the counselor might suggest steps the couple can take to avoid being pulled into familiar and counterproductive sequences or to support alternative patterns of interacting. In ending the session the counselor wants to allow enough time to bring the appointment to a close and, in doing so, consider possibilities for keeping therapeutic change alive for the couple in the intervening week.

Summary

In this chapter we have provided an outline for the initial and follow-up couples counseling sessions. Of course, no outline should be rigidly adhered to and counselors need to rely on their clinical wisdom and knowledge to adequately respond to the needs of their clients. With this in mind, however, it is our belief that conceptualizing the flow of the counseling session, with allowance for possible modifications, can provide for a therapeutic structure which may facilitate couples counseling.

4

Motivational Interventions

We focus our interventions around therapeutic issues in the areas of motivation, meaning and management, and in the next four chapters each of these issues will be discussed. When couples are motivated to maintain or improve their relationship, have a satisfying understanding of the dynamics, influencing factors, and values within their relationship, and possess the behavioral management skills which allow them to negotiate problems in their relationship, they usually have a self-image of success. Life 'makes sense' to them and they see themselves as coping satisfactorily. Such couples have a commitment to solving life's problems and a sense of confidence or understanding that they can handle the pitfalls of life that will come their way.

Of the three intervention areas, motivation, meaning, and management, the first area of assessment and intervention is motivation. Engagement in the counseling process requires that participants find the activity and potential outcomes of counseling meaningful. Motivation to work on the relationship is an essential component in the equation for successful outcomes in couples counseling and is linked to a sense of hope that the relationship can improve. Usually when couples seek counseling the level of motivation and hope is disparate between them. One member often presents as though they want the relationship to continue while the other is more distant and doubtful about its continuation.

Motivation is important to any successful endeavor, including and perhaps especially long-term and intimate relationships. Hope, an essential element of motivation, has been conceptualized by Miller and Powers as an 'anticipation of a continued good state, an improved state, or a release from a perceived entrapment' (1988: 6). Their definition speaks directly to the atmosphere that must be generated if couples counseling is to be successful. The anticipation of a continued good state usually comes during a latter stage of counseling, whereas release from perceived entrapment or looking forward to an improved state are conditions that must be addressed earlier in the counseling process.

The Winners, Mel and Sue, first came to counseling because their sons, Timmy aged 22 and Paul aged 20, were not making a transition to adulthood. The two boys were pals, they drank and drove, they wouldn't stay in college, and they wouldn't take jobs. They lived at home and assumed little responsibility but they did assume a lot of privileges. Sue was angry with the boys and yet she adored them. Mel was somewhat like the boys himself, a man's man who played golf, stopped at the bar after work on Fridays, flirted with the secretaries and kept his wife a bit on guard. She in return kept herself looking nice and flirted a bit with available males. Their relationship was symmetrical in that they each increased their flirting when they wanted to have interaction with the other. This system produced jealousy but also interest and excitement. In public, the Winners would look to some romantics like the perfect couple. They dressed like 16-year-old farm kids going steady for the first time, with matching plaid shirts, matching blue jeans and matching boots. They were attentive with each other and yet it always seemed that their coupleness was intended to be a joint flirting exhibition. It was as though Mel was saying to other women, 'Look at what a sensitive guy I am. Wouldn't it be nice to have a guy like me?' and Sue was giving a similar message about being attentive and sexy. She too seemed to be sending a message to others about how nice or exciting it would be to relate to her. The boundary around the couple was always ambiguous and, so, it appeared that they experienced limited hope for the marriage as well as little motivation for developing the relationship.

The case of Mel and Sue Winner illustrates dimensions of motivation and hope that are initially present in many of the couples we see. Mel and Sue's initial complaint focused on their sons' behavior and the sense that they were their sons' prisoners. They couldn't leave them alone at home or the boys would take their cars, have girls over or throw a rowdy party. They didn't see the boys making any progress and the future looked dim. Again, Mel and Sue's sense of hope and a resultant feeling of motivation was low. With regard to parenting, they felt trapped, didn't believe life was good and didn't see it getting better. The first therapeutic task was to wean the parents and boys from each other. As this task was proceeding elements of the couple's relationship arose. Sue talked of her anger with Mel and her feeling of being trapped because she didn't have appropriate job skills. Mel shared concerns that he had not shared before because he was afraid Sue would not respond. The counselor framed their release of anxiety and anger as concern for the relationship. Developing a perception of shared caring for the relationship allowed Mel and Sue to start planning for the family's future. Planning efforts can be one of the early signals that the couple have become more motivated to work on the relationship. Indeed, the Winners' cognitive understanding of their marriage did not appear to have grown much but their verbal reports began to indicate that they felt listened to and cared about and they expressed a renewed hope about their relationship.

Beliefs held by counselors about the purposes of their role when working with couples as well as the images they hold about relationships can either be motivating or result in despair. Successful counselors have a repertoire of ways of thinking about the structures and situations couples present to them. They also have a variety of responses and techniques to use in addressing the circumstances that couples present. This library of contexts and responses has usually been developed through experience, reflection, and study. A part of this library of contexts and therapeutic responses needs to be focused on contributing to the hope and motivation in couples' lives. In offering hope the counselor is attempting to establish an atmosphere of learning and adventure, and we have found it more productive to help the couple commit to the adventure of seeing how good they can make their relationship rather than committing to the relationship itself or to their partner. The couple do not feel trapped by such a commitment and are more likely to focus on the work of couples counseling. In creating a hopeful atmosphere we have defined three major paths of motivational interventions: communication; observation, reflection, and meaning; and action (see Figure 4.1).

Communication

Distressed couples and counselors report communication as a problem in their relationship more frequently than any other area of concern (Geiss & O'Leary, 1981). What couples mean when they speak of communication problems may be vastly different from what the counselor hears. Usually the complaining member means, 'My spouse does not hear me and respond in a way that I'd like.' Little attention is usually given to listening. The communication trail has three paths that offer hope and motivation to couples who feel trapped and without a future. These paths include counselor listening, communication skills training, and trust creation.

Communication
  Counselor listening
  Couple communication skills training
  Creating trustable perceptions and behavior

Observation, reflection, and meaning
  Developing a sense of humor
  Reviewing video tapes
  Finding hopeful rays of sunshine
  Highlighting points of efficacy
  Separating present from past
  Using language of hope
  Inviting the couple to dream

Action
  Pretending to change behavior
  Finding options
  Using community to enrich the relationship

Figure 4.1 *Paths of offering hope and motivation*

Counselor Listening

Usually when couples come to counseling, neither has been seriously listened to for some time. The counselor who listens kindly and carefully to what is said and unsaid, what is felt and what is hidden, to disappointments and dreams, to wishes and fears, conveys a sense of worthwhileness to clients. Couples respond to such listening by revealing themselves more fully and by thinking of themselves as interesting and valuable. Beavers and Kaslow (1981) noted that when counselors listen carefully to clients and convey that they genuinely want to be of assistance the ascendance from pessimism to optimism is often activated. Listening is a critical attitude and skill for counselors to possess. The following phrases may be of assistance in conveying to the couple that they are being taken seriously.

- You felt/feel _____.
- You thought/think _____.
- I hear you saying _____.
- What did you feel when _____ happened?
- What did you think when _____ happened?
- What do you do when _____ happens?
- How did you react to/cope with _____?
- You are feeling _____ about.
- You think he/she is going to _____.

Many couples who seek counseling have experienced chaotic childhoods where alcohol, violence, and neglect were common. Often it appears intimate relationships are stimulated by one individual sensing a like-kindness with their partner and a desire to develop a relationship different from their past. In such instances, experiencing an empathic caring individual is an uplifting experience. The transfer of communication skills from the counselor to the couple seldom happens by unacknowledged modeling. Consequently, couples often must be directed to the hopeful path of communication skills.

Couple Communication Skills Training

A usual scenario in starting counseling with a couple is to have them describe the problem(s) they have in their relationship. After one member reports the problems, the other often provides the 'correct' version. What ensues, if the counselor does not provide control, is a verbal donnybrook of uninsightful talk and a dearth of listening. One of the indicators of success in counseling occurs when a couple's conversation conveys consideration and acceptance of both partners' thoughts and feelings. Sometimes this transformation from acrimony to synergy occurs as a result of just talking. Frequently, however, helpful communication is encouraged by the establishment of some communication rules and guidelines – some boundaries in the relationship. Once helpful talking and listening are taking place the couple experience the hope that comes from release and anticipation of a better state and, as a result, motivation for working on the relationship seems to be increased.

As with the implementation of many interventions, prior work is needed to increase the chances of success of the communication skills training. Couples must move from being what de Shazer (1988) terms visitors or complainers to customers. Both acknowledgement of a problem and the expression of a desire to be involved in doing something about the problem are critical before an intervention is proposed.

In the middle of or after a nonproductive communication exchange is the perfect time for a counselor to introduce the idea of communication skills training. The focus is on helping couples to be good speakers and listeners. The goal is to help the couple to understand that helpful communication involves learning to speak and listen in ways that increase shared understanding and mutual problem solving. The counselor needs to encourage a view that productive communication is a process of mutual benefit rather than a power struggle or debate. During the communication training process the counselor serves as a rule setter, enforcer, and coach who explains and perhaps demonstrates behaviors that make for rewarding exchanges. The following dialogue serves as a model for introducing the communication skills training.

Counselor: Let me stop you for a second. This doesn't seem to be going well, does it?

John: No.

Mary: Not at all.

Counselor: Is this how it goes when you are having problems talking to each other?

Mary: Yup.

John: Just like this.

Counselor: Would you like it to go differently? What about you, John?

John: You bet.

Counselor: How about you, Mary?

Mary: Sure.

Counselor: Are you each willing to do something different to see if you can make it better?

John: Okay.

Mary: Sure.

Counselor: All right then. This may seem a bit artificial, at least for a while, but we are going to practice talking and listening with some basic rules. We use rules when we play many games so that the game is fair to all and so that all enjoy playing. The rules I am going to give you are much like that, they will help you communicate for your mutual benefit. There are a few rules for the speaker and a few more for the listener and you will take turns being speaker and listener. Who wants to start by being the speaker?

Mary: I will.

Counselor: Okay. Mary, I want you to tell John what you think and feel about the childcare situation you were just discussing. Talk about yourself and about what you want and feel rather than talking about what John does or doesn't do. Say, 'I'm really tired. I'd like you to take care of the kids tomorrow' rather than, 'You never think of me. You never pitch in and help out with the kids.' Do you see the difference?

Mary: Yes.

Counselor: Now, John, as the listener you have the tough task. You have two jobs. First, I want you to find out as much as possible about what Mary thinks and feels about the childcare situation. Part of the listener's job is to find out as much as you can. This may be hard because Mary may say things that you get mad about or that you believe are wrong. I don't think it will be hard though if you commit yourself to listening, understanding, and asking questions.

Now, secondly, Mary is going to have three minutes to talk and when she is finished I want you to summarize what she said and what you think she felt. Mary will then indicate whether you left anything out. Then we will switch roles and John, you will be the speaker and Mary, you will be the listener. Do you understand? [*Nods*] Mary, begin by telling John what you think and feel about the childcare situation.

The counselor's role now becomes that of a coach during the conversation. As a coach the counselor makes sure that thoughts and feelings are clearly expressed and that the recipient of the message works at improving her or his listening skills. Here is an example of rules to keep in mind when coaching a couple in communication skills training:

1   Talk about what you want or feel rather than what your partner doesn't do.
2   Make clear statements, 'I want us to have more time together on the weekends' instead of ambiguous statements, 'I just wish we were happier.'
3   As the listener, be able to summarize what your partner thinks and feels.
4   Stay focused on an issue, don't get sidetracked onto unrelated issues.
5   Don't monopolize the talk time, save your partner time to respond.
6   Avoid threats, 'If this doesn't change I'm leaving.'

When the exercise is completed the counselor can help the couple learn from the activity by asking them what they liked and did not like and by helping them notice the differences in their own behavior during the activity compared to their prior 'discussion.' The raising of satisfying differences is encouraging with couples who think that behavior cannot change. Successful in-session activities usually raise questions concerning trust: trust of self and trust of one's partner. The self-talk may be, 'We just talked to each other but I doubt we will be able to continue the behavior.' Trust is an important component of being hopeful.

Creating Trustable Perceptions and Behavior
Trust is an important aspect in the cultivation of hope and motivation. To trust implies an expectation that another can be depended

upon to act in the best interest of the relationship or spouse, or at least not to act in a way that harms the relationship or spouse. It is helpful to refocus the trust issue into an active rather than a passive or acted-upon framework. This refocused framework, trying not to do unto others what you would not have them do unto you (Kohlberg, 1971), asks each partner to answer the question, 'What would it be like to be married to me?' (Piercy, 1991). The effect of a serious response to the question is usually the creation of a shared reality for the couple. Such a shared reality serves as a basis for trust and consequently for hope.

Perhaps an example of trust leading to hope and motivation for working on the relationship would be helpful.

Heather and Sam had been married for less than a year. Sam worked long hours, sometimes not even coming home at night. He claimed he slept in his office or sometimes in his car. He had his paycheck directly deposited into an account that did not include Heather's name and brought 'cash' to Heather whenever it was time to pay the bills. He also had a number of personal and expensive hobbies, a race car, a sports car, etc., that did not include Heather. Heather, naturally, was always pushing Sam to let her in on his secret world. She wondered why he had not gotten around to changing the bank account to include her, where he was at night, and why he had not given up some of his 'childish' interests. Her wonderings took the form of complaints to which Sam responded by complaining about her 'nagging.' The couple were caught in a vicious cycle of attack and counterattack that was far removed from the core issue of accommodation and trust in the relationship. Having them carefully answer the question, 'What would it be like to be married to me?' allowed each to acknowledge their own contribution to the distrustful and painful atmosphere in their relationship. The question, asked by the counselor, allowed each to confess and experience their own contribution to the problem in a manner that was not possible when the accusations were being made by their spouse. The result was threefold. Each was validated by hearing that their own view of the relationship was seen as being accurate by their spouse. Secondly, each was able to acknowledge the role they were playing in the distress they were experiencing. Finally, the shared, trustable, perspective and the refocusing from blaming to acceptance of responsibility for contributing to the problems led to positive change: bank accounts being changed, informing each other more carefully about schedules, etc. These new 'trustable' behaviors rekindled a sense of hope.

The building of trust and concomitant reduction of mistrust can actually serve as an evaluative indicator of how well the counseling is going. However, the mistrust held by one or both spouses is often deepseated. The mistrust may be coupled with an almost childlike uncritical trust or desire to trust others (Beavers & Kaslow, 1981). Such a client will say, 'Every time I trust her/him they take advantage of me' or 'I'm always getting stepped on.' Such a statement often emanates from an individual who has a strong desire to be relieved of the 'burdens' of life. In such instances the relief may be provided by marrying a 'prince' or 'princess.' Such a strong need for 'relief' often feeds the desire for blind trust which sets the scene for being hurt. The hurt then reinforces the mistrust, hopelessness, and despair. In a case referred to in the first chapter, Sue and Tom were married after a three-month courtship. About eight months into the marriage Sue sought counseling because she realized the marriage was a bad mistake. The couple had experienced financial difficulties from the beginning of their marriage and Sue had just discovered that her husband did not work and that he had not worked as long as she had known him. Perhaps the brevity of the courtship was an indicator of a strong desire on the part of one or both parties to 'solve' some problem in life by marrying a 'prince' or 'princess'.

Other manifestations of this trust–mistrust syndrome occur with people who are surprised to learn that their partner is an alcoholic or that they have a criminal record. In such instances the cultivation of a middle ground of trust or differentiated trust is helpful. In these cases counseling may need to focus on developing a self-trust and on maintaining some skepticism towards one's partner. Such skepticism can be framed as giving the relationship a 'high priority' (Piercy, 1991). Blind trust, on the other hand, would mean the relationship had a low priority; that is, the relationship really didn't need to be attended to. For example, in an instance where alcohol has been a problem it is sometimes helpful for the counselor to address the blind trust–mistrust cycle by saying in the presence of both partners, 'You know, Mary, I think you would like to believe that Bob will never drink again. You've had that trust before. But there is a part of you that will always be a little doubtful, a little fearful that these bad times are not over. I think it is important to trust yourself and to be a little doubtful.' The goal here is to help the client develop a healthy trust, one which is relative and selective.

The development of selectivity relative to objects and moments of trust involves the acquisition of a new skill for many clients. Clients low in trust tend to generalize about their negative involvement with others. Their beliefs follow catastrophic patterns (Dattilio & Padesky, 1990): 'Everything always ends up bad,' 'People take advantage of you,' 'Men just want to use you,' etc. Often people who hold these 'absolute' views are involved in cycles of behavior that reinforce their views. These destructive behavior cycles also include selective perceptions whereby one sees behavior selectively and interprets it in a way that reinforces basic cognitions about life. Relative to trust, the counselor's task is to help the couple recognize exceptions to their basic views. In a fashion, this recognition of exceptions (de Shazer, 1988) helps to confuse one's usual way of viewing life. Instead of seeing life just as black and white one now sees shades of gray. In addition to assisting clients in recognizing that there are exceptions to their basic views of life, de Shazer indicated that the exceptions have to make a difference to the client. That is, the differences that are pointed to must be differences that have some meaning or importance to the client.

A case example might clarify how providing exceptions to a perspective can help increase hope as well as motivation to work on the relationship.

Jan and Mike had been married for 12 years. They came to counseling because Mike had just discovered that Jan was seeing another guy. Mike reported that he had feared Jan would always run off with someone else. Mike had not gone to college while Jan had completed a degree in business. Mike indicated that he thought Jan had married him because she felt sorry for him and trapped into the relationship. She had broken off the engagement about a year prior to the established wedding date and she had returned to Mike after dating others for about three months. Mike believed she had only returned because he was so upset over the breaking of the engagement. For about the past six years Mike had developed interests away from Jan because he wanted to 'be ready' if Jan decided to leave him. Jan had taken a job about two years prior to counseling, and during that time she had become interested in a coworker who was attentive to her and seemed to be self-assured. These latter two points of Jan's wanting more attention and wanting a relationship with someone who was more self-assured (so didn't need reassurance from her) were critical in the intervention process.

The therapeutic perspective was to define the times of

turmoil in the relationship (the break-up during the engagement period and the recent attraction of Jan to another man) as being the exceptions to a pattern of commitment and love. This view was taken because of the long reported history of a satisfying marriage and the similarity in the dynamics of the two situations of reported stress. The following transcript shows how the counselor was able to define the marriage as a loving and stable relationship and that difficulties really occurred as rare exceptions. This interpretation was counter to Mike's view that the marriage was always tenuous.

Counselor: Jan, what first attracted you to Mike? What did you first like about him?

Jan: Well, we met when I was a freshman in college and although Mike was only a year older, he already had a job, was out living on his own, and was making a good salary.

Counselor: He really knew what he wanted and you liked that.

Jan: Yea, he was different from other guys my age who were so caught up in themselves, always showing off. He was much more settled, looking to the future and so supportive.

Counselor: What happened that caused you to break your engagement?

Jan: It happened when I was a senior and I'm not sure. Mike just seemed to get quiet, stayed away. We stopped having fun.

Counselor: What was going on for you, Mike?

Mike: I don't know. I guess I sort of felt like we had fun and I'd tried to push Jan along so we would get married before her senior year, but she didn't want to. I began to think she didn't want to get married and I got scared and just kept to myself waiting for her to end it and she eventually did. I felt like she had used me for three years and that now she would move on to something better.

Jan: I didn't know what else to do. I didn't really want to end it but Mike changed so much that I didn't know what to do.

Counselor: What was going on for the two of you about two years ago?

Mike: Well, Jan took a job. We'd talked about it for a while. Our kids were getting older and Jan felt like she wanted to use some of her skills a little more.

Counselor: How did you feel about Jan working outside the home?

Mike: Oh, I wanted her to. She went to college and she really had never gotten to use her degree.

Counselor: Did anything worry you about Jan going to work?

Mike: Oh, a little. I had a little fear that she would get all excited about work and lose interest in me.

Counselor: What did you do?

Mike: That seemed pretty childish to me so I just kept it to myself.

Counselor: Did you do anything else?

Mike: I just tried to be encouraging to her and kept busy.

Counselor: What do you make of what you have just heard?

Jan: You know, what I see is that Mike gets anxious and withdraws and when he does I feel abandoned.

Counselor: Yes, I see that too and it seems like that has happened at times when both of you are going to make changes. It happened when Jan graduated from college and it seems that you, Mike, might have thought she was better than you and didn't need you. It happened again when the two of you anticipated Jan's going back to work. It was almost that Mike thought, 'Now she's going to discover there are a lot more exciting men out there.' Both times you stopped being who you are, that person Jan really loves, a considerate guy who attends to her and a guy that really knows where he is going. Does that seem accurate?

Jan and Mike: Yea.

Counselor: But those two times seem like real exceptions. For twelve, really about sixteen years, except for two brief times you have had a very caring relationship. I don't think that could have happened unless you both loved each other very much.

[*Jan and Mike: both smiled and Mike appeared more relaxed.*]

Usually the search for exceptions that build trust and consequently hope and motivation is much more direct than the above. Often the exceptions may be generated by direct questions.

- You say Mary is never on time, when was the last time she was prompt?
- You don't think Bill ever cares about you. Has there been any exception to that in the past month?

If the counselor keeps the spouse on task by focusing on exceptions, almost without fail one partner will generate examples that challenge the view that their mate is completely untrustworthy. The counselor does, however, want to help each partner to be realistic in their views of their mate and their relationship.

Hope and motivation to work on the relationship can only exist in an atmosphere of trust. Trustability must be believably communicated for one to anticipate a favorable future. These three communication paths, counselor listening, communication skills training, and trustable perception and behavior, represent three of the paths available for counselors to help build hope and motivation back into the couple's relationship.

Observation, Reflection, and Meaning

Couples who come for counseling live in a shrunken world. Their lives are caught in the pain of losing, of planning their next attack, of bitterness and frustration. When the relationship is going badly there is often no world beyond the conflictual pattern of interaction. Other than being involved in an affair, perhaps, there is often little meaningful involvement with work, friends, family, hobbies or self-care. The energy of the couple is tied up in emotional conflict. Hope returns to the relationship when one or both partners can be coaxed into seeing things differently, viewing their spouse's or their own behavior more benevolently, and taking a more creative approach to their relationship.

A step in helping couples to see themselves differently and more hopefully can be taken by assisting them in observing themselves and their relationship. When the counselor is able to assist in transforming the relationship from an offensive and defensive struggle to an observing and learning unit a corner has been turned (Guerin et al., 1987). Such training of observation skills can often be stimulated by the counselor asking appropriate questions or making observations. Couples always react to each other but seldom are they aware of the behavior to which they are reacting. As a way of bringing the stimulus behavior to a conscious level the counselor might say:

- What are you thinking/feeling right now?
- What do you think your partner is thinking/feeling right now?
- I think your partner just dropped out, ask her/him what they are thinking/feeling.
- It seems that when you talk for more than fifteen seconds, which happens frequently, your partner withdraws.
- Perhaps in an effort to get your partner to hear you, you say the same thing about three different ways. When you do she/he seems to tune out.
- Did you notice that the quieter you get the louder your partner gets?
- When she/he gives that speech what are you supposed to do next?

Any of these observations set the stage for experiments in change. By simply providing a directive the counselor can induce change. For example, the counselor might say to the withdrawing partner, 'When she gets loud I'd like for you to stand up, tell her how you feel, what you think, etc. I'll let you know what to do.' Hope rises when the couple sense that they have control over that which was previously beyond control. We will now introduce seven counseling interventions that lie along the observation, reflection and meaning path leading toward increased hope and motivation for an improved relationship.

Developing a Sense of Humor

A developing sense of humor is also a symptom of a growing ability to observe. To find something humorous or to enjoy a spontaneous chuckle implies an underlying ability to observe. The courage to view oneself or the relationship as humorous is often a sign of hope. On the other hand, to report one's spouse as funny is often a sign of frustration and may need to be addressed as destructive communication; however, the counselor may encourage humor in the couple by making metaphorical reference to their behavior. For example, to the quarreling couple the counselor might say, 'You remind me of two of the three stooges. First one of you sticks your fingers in the other's eyes, then the other pours water on your head.' The next time this aggression and counteraggression appears the counselor can say, 'I'm not sure, are you pouring water or sticking your fingers in her/his eyes.' The counselor's focus is on helping the couple to observe their behavior while also providing a humorous framework in which to interpret the observation. Humor brings a lifting of spirit and a renewed sense of hope.

Reviewing Videotaped Sessions

Reviewing with the couple critical incidents of videotaped sessions can increase their observational skills and resultantly increase their sense of hope. Playing back 'successful' interactions is especially encouraging. These segments can be processed by asking the couple to comment on what they liked about the interaction in the tape. Specifically, the counselor might ask, 'What did you like that your spouse said or did in that segment? What did you say or do that you thought was helpful and/or felt good to you?' Again, elements of observation and control are increased for the couple and consequently hope is renewed.

Finding Hopeful Rays of Sunshine

The world that the distressed couple observe is often one-sided, dark and shadowy. Counselors can assist couples in finding the hopeful rays of sunshine (Beavers & Kaslow, 1981) amidst the clouds. One way of finding these rays is by asking a variation of one of de Shazer's (1988) skeleton key questions. Here, the counselor inquires about what happened this week to give the couple a moment of hope. Helping the couple to be specific about 'what happened' is important if there is to be a conscious continuation of the event. At other times celebrating a positive trend or event by exposing an observation can assist a couple in increasing their optimism. Comments like, 'You seemed to take it easier in your relationship today' or 'You reported three good days this week versus none last week' may help a couple experience a surge of satisfaction and hope.

As with most interventions, timing and the relative position the counselor takes in noting rays of sunshine are critical in helping the couple to bask in the sunshine. Pointing out positive aspects of the relationship 'too early' in counseling often produces resistance on the part of couples. It may appear to them that the counselor is taking their problems too lightly or that she or he does not understand the extent of their pain. At times, it seems that the couple show more severe symptoms as a way of helping the counselor understand the magnitude of their presenting problem. It also seems that more humble comments by the counselor are often more acceptable to the couple than are comments that shed light on the counselor's observational skills. The following prefacing comments to the 'ray of sunshine' statement can be helpful in gaining acceptance by the couple.

- I could be wrong, but it seems the two of you . . .
- I'm not sure, but the two of you . . .
- I don't know, but there seems to be a little something new in your relationship . . .

Finally, it appears to us that 'rays of sunshine' are more helpful, at least during early and middle stages of counseling, when they are aimed at celebrating aspects of the couple's relationship rather than celebrating aspects of one of the two partners. During initial phases of counseling, celebrating individual victories often produces a resistive or jealous response from the other partner. Although this response can be used therapeutically, the dynamic involved where one partner feels inferior to the other does not engender hope.

Highlighting Points of Efficacy

While rays of sunshine focus on positive aspects in the couple's relationship, the highlighting of points of efficacy focuses on specific effective actions taken by either member of the relationship. The sense of hope comes from the perception of one partner that what they said or did seemed to be 'right.' The question, 'What did you do this week that you felt pleased about?' will often produce a response wherein one partner reports a new behavior that they felt good about. This new behavior renews hope by helping the person to see that new behavior is possible.

Carl and Linda had been married for five tumultuous years. At times when Linda felt angry and insecure she would tell Carl that she wanted a divorce. Carl would then reassure Linda by telling her how much he loved her and how much he wanted to stay married. Such an exchange returned their relationship to a stable form but did not help them grow beyond the pattern of distancing and feeling distanced, and threatening and reconciliation. The couple finally came to counseling a short time after Linda had once again threatened Carl with a divorce and he had responded, not by saying, 'I'm sorry' but by saying, 'If you really feel that way, maybe we had better go ahead and get one.' This new behavior had opened the relationship to the potential for change. When the counselor asked Carl how it felt to change his behavior Carl indicated that it felt good. He felt like he was no longer imprisoned or locked in to having to dance when Linda threatened. Referring back to Miller and Powers' (1988) definition of hope, Carl felt released from entrapment. Henceforth, Carl became more involved in the relationship, which is what Linda had been seeking via her ill-judged ultimatum. Together they became more effective in solving the issues of their relationship.

In finding points of efficacy, the counselor is seeking to empower the spouses, by noting and celebrating new and adaptive behavior. The acknowledged behavior may occur in any areas of the life of one or both members of the relationship. Often a spark may be struck in a project at work, in the alteration of a relationship with another family member, in beginning an exercise and/or weight loss program, or in beginning or terminating a hobby or leisure activity. From a systems perspective these changes are both symptomatic of and stimuli for new life within the couple's relationship.

Separating the Present from the Past

Another area of hope along the observation, reflection, and meaning path can be found in distinguishing the now from the then (Beavers & Kaslow, 1981). The focus in couples counseling is usually on the here and now, on problem definition, problem maintenance, and solution-focused strategies. Frequently, however, the counselor will note an emotional response in one or both partners that appears to be beyond that provided by the moment or even the history of the relationship. At such times it may be helpful for the counselor to inquire, 'What other event in your life reminds you of what is going on now in your relationship?' Recognition of the previous event(s) may start a process of boundary making that is liberating and hope-producing by separating the past from the present.

> Frank and Susan had been married for 11 years and had daughters 9, 6, and 4 years of age. In the past year Susan had become highly critical of Frank's relationship with their older daughter. She was concerned about their spending time alone together and insinuated that inappropriate behavior might be taking place between Frank and the nine-year-old. Such concerns must be taken seriously by counselors. However, when the family was seen as a whole there had been no evidence of inappropriate behavior between Frank and the girls. The mother was so concerned that she had previously had the daughter seen by a counselor. A check with this counselor and the school counselor did not discover cause for alarm about the relationship between father and daughter. Inquiry with Susan concerning her own childhood revealed that her father had an incestual relationship with her for a two-year period beginning when she was nine years old. She had never told Frank of this experience and feared he would kill her father and be quite angry with her. The outcome of her disclosure was that Frank was quite understanding. Susan joined an incest survivors group and made rapid progress in separating the past events in her own life from the present events in her own and her husband's life.

Such cases involving emotional and behavioral residue are often long-term and progress is often slower than in the case of Frank and Susan. This slowness of progress is sometimes evident because the present and past have a great deal of similarity. This is especially true where physical, sexual, or substance abuse are present. Still a differentiation between the present and the past, particularly in terms of the developmental level of the couple, will provide a starting point for counseling. For the counselor to reinforce the idea that the spouses are now adults, and can therefore expect different things from themselves and act in different ways than they did as children and adolescents, may provide enough differentiation and empowerment for them to begin behaving in a more responsible adult-like manner rather than as powerless children. Such an observation and reflection may assist them in assuming more meaningful roles in their relationship.

Using the Language of Hope

A sixth trail of hope along the observation, reflection, and meaning path involves the counselor's use of the language of hope, the labeling of life in a way that energizes the couple. In counseling, couples often label their own or their partner's behavior in an absolute or hopeless fashion. The relabeling (Minuchin & Fishman, 1981) of this absolute, negative view will often allow the couple the maneuverability (freedom from entrapment) they need to be released from the bondage of their current relationship. In stimulating hope, the new labels usually have a positive connotation and involve an alternative truth (Weeks & L'Abate, 1982). In relabeling the counselor is usually attempting to define the client's motives or goals as positive but their means or behaviors as misinformed (Haley, 1963). A somewhat stereotypical example of this last point is the couple engaged in complementary behavior where one talks incessantly and the other withdraws. The goal may be labeled positively as seeking closeness but the means produce the opposite effect. The more one talks to gain the involvement of the other, the more the other withdraws to quiet their spouse. This cycle of behavior only heightens the complementarity.

A number of writers have provided 'helpful' hopeful labels for common paralyzing labels provided by couples (Landfield & Rivers, 1975; Weeks & L'Abate, 1982; Weeks, 1977). The following 'labels' and 'relabels' are provided to assist counselors in stimulating hope in couples.

- withdrawn – thoughtful, cautious
- passive – accepting
- angry – involved
- stubborn – steadfast, committed, stable
- seductive – desire to be liked
- oppositional – independent, strong individual
- oversensitive – aware
- insensitive – protecting oneself

- submissive – able to be a team member, cooperative
- critical – open, forthright
- digressing – exploring possibilities
- immature – fun-loving

The counselor's ability to hear the paralyzing and homeostatic labels used by clients and to supply new labels that provide a new meaning allows for flexibility of response and a renewal of hope.

Inviting the Couple to Dream
The last trail in finding hope through observation, reflection, and meaning is that of issuing an invitation to the couple to dream and live new dreams or to renew old dreams. Joseph Campbell (1988) indicated that what people are seeking is not the meaning of life but rather the experience of being alive. Distressed couples often speak of feeling lifeless, going through the motions, being burned-out and uncaring. They are not caught up in life. A part of what we do as counselors is to help this world by teaching people how to live in it. We assist people in gaining a deeper awareness of the act of living itself. This deeper awareness of the act of living is reflected in the following:

> *Counselor*: You say your relationship has been better this week. Why has it gone better?
>
> *Shelley*: I went home from the last session and I thought about it and I said, 'I really love this guy. Why am I badgering him and complaining all the time?' Once I got that through my head it was easy to enjoy our relationship and even get on with doing fun things in my life.

Counselors help couples to establish priorities and to pursue that which is truly important in their lives. We would believe prioritization occurs in Strategic Therapy (Madanes, 1981) when an intervention has stopped a troubling behavior pattern and one or other of the partners now says, 'What is really bothering me is . . .' The utility of the strategic intervention is in eliminating the symptom the couple used as a detour for other issues in their life. Without the detour the couple could begin to encounter each other. Such encounter is to experience being alive. Much of what was stated above under the hopeful path of communication is about helping couples to share their hopes and needs. Such intimate sharing of pain and joy is an experience of being alive.

Counselors can also assist couples to experience being alive by inviting them to dream. Just as goals of counseling need to reflect the couple's goals, the dreams of counseling need to be the couple's dreams. The counselor's role is to help to create an atmosphere in which dreaming is possible. This atmosphere can best be created at times when the couple's agendas are not pressing. Usually the dream phase occurs after the crisis that brought the couple to counseling has been relieved. The sequence for encouraging the invention of a meaningful future goes from dream preparation to dreaming to processing the dream(s). The counselor can introduce the session by saying something like:

Counselor: You have really been working hard and today I'd like to change the tempo a bit. I'd like you to think a bit about the future. Does that seem okay with you?

This question helps to make sure that the proposed agenda is acceptable to the clients.

Counselor: To help you to get to your vision of the future I'd like you to close your eyes and relax.

At this point a relaxation exercise is used.

Counselor: I'd like you to imagine that counseling has been successful and the two of you have found solutions to the problems you are having. You are looking forward to your life together and to your individual lives. What do you notice that is different for you: in your relationship [*Pause*]; at home [*Pause*]; with your families; at work; in your leisure time; and in taking care of yourself?

The particular realms of the future vision can be altered to fit the needs of the couple. It is helpful for the couple to write a few notes about their dreams before they verbally report their dream to their spouse. The note taking allows them to maintain the separateness of their dreams. Allow each spouse five minutes to report their vision of the future. The counselor's focus during this time should be on helping the reporter to tell her or his story and on assuring that the listener hears the dream.

The dream-processing phase can be implemented by asking the couple to note similarities and differences in the dreams. Similarities and differences may be about content, elements of time, the language used to report the vision, and the manner of delivery. If a hopeful tone is desired the counselor will focus on similarities, the acceptability of differences, and the uniqueness of the contributions of the individuals. Sometimes, it is helpful to ask the couple what was surprising to them about their spouse's dream. Couples often take this time of dreaming to reveal a hidden desire. These surprises may be about having a baby, changing a job, going to work, moving, etc. Asking what each of them liked about their own and their partner's dream encourages a sense of cooperation. Dislikes should also be noted.

If the couple are in a cooperative, working phase the processing can proceed by asking each of the partners what they need to do to bring their dream to life. What do they need in order to complete their dream? What do they need from their spouse to complete their dream? Further processing can take a problem-solving approach that is more action-oriented.

Astute counselors can also reveal the hopes of individual partners by listening to the assumptions behind their comments. When spouses are angry with each other, each harbors a dream about life that is discrepant with how they are experiencing life at the moment. Revelation of these assumptions will allow exploration of their validity.

Bernard and Connie had been married 7 years and had two children 5 and 3 years of age. Both Bernard and Connie had been employed throughout their marriage. Bernard was continually critical of Connie's parenting behavior and he also expressed doubt that they were giving the children the attention they needed and deserved. However, he made little effort to become more involved with the children. When asked to share the dream he had of married life at the time he and Connie were married, Bernard envisioned Connie working until the children were born and then leaving work to devote herself to the children and to him. The discrepancy between his dream and the reality of their lives left Bernard feeling frustrated. He manifested this frustration by being critical of Connie and in a sense blaming her for the situation. As discussion progressed, Bernard admitted that he liked some aspects of the life style that he and Connie were permitted by having two incomes. He also mentioned that he was proud of Connie and her ability to both work and contribute. Over the next few weeks, as Bernard and Connie dreamed a new dream, Bernard became more involved in the family. No longer did he speak of having to help Connie with the family, but rather, he bought into the partnership by making real contributions. The development of a new myth for Bernard and Connie was facilitated because the counselor heard the old myth expressed in the assumptions underlying Bernard's presenting complaint. The couple through the revelation of the dream was moved from talking about the meaning of life to the experience of living.

Action

The experience of life points to the last of the three major paths of hope and motivation and that happens to be the path of action. To take an action will often raise hope because it relieves the doldrums of feeling stuck or trapped. The three action paths that we will discuss include pretending to change behavior, finding options, and using the community to enrich the relationship.

Pretending to Change Behavior

Many family practitioners have stressed the importance of doing over that of understanding (Fisch, Weakland, & Segal, 1982; Haley, 1990). They emphasize the importance of doing something different to break patterns of homeostatic behavior. The importance of getting clients to change behavior, if only by pretending to change behavior, has been stressed by Madanes (1981) and Mosak and Dreikurs (1973). Mosak and Dreikurs were suggesting that people may become that which they pretend to be. In other words, the first step of being is pretending. When the counselor requests the client(s) to engage in pretend behavior she or he is acknowledging that they may not feel like actually doing the behavior but they will be willing to engage in it under a pretense. Thus client resistance can often be avoided. For example, we might say to a client, 'Bob, I doubt that you feel much like showing your wife affection, but I want you to show her affection this week on three occasions. Don't worry about whether you mean it or not, but I do want you to do it in such a way that she can't tell whether you are pretending or not.' Such a directive acknowledges the client's feelings and yet stimulates new behavior. It is the new action that will often stimulate a different tone in the relationship. Thus the path of hopeful action involves getting couples to do something different.

Finding Options

Finding options is another action-oriented path for increasing hope and motivation. Often in discussing options couples either do not see that they have options or upon raising options they immediately generate reasons why the options cannot be pursued. At such times the counselor can be helpful by simply asking the couple to do something different. Steve de Shazer (1985) has discussed this type of intervention at some length. We have found that the directive to do something different can be potent when introduced during a counseling session in which the couple are caught in a homeostatic conflict. The counselor might introduce the directive by saying,

> *Counselor*: You seem like you are stuck again. We've seen this before where each of you seems more bent on attacking and defeating the other than on solving a problem. Do you agree? Would you like to change this? Okay. We have 20 more minutes in the session and I want you to think for a second how you want to be at the end of the hour. Now I want you to make this come out differently. Do something different. Go ahead.

Usually, the couple will cycle into an old pattern of behavior at this point and the counselor can keep them on task by stating, 'I'm not sure, this seems like the same thing. Do something different.' Or, the counselor might ask, 'Is this the same or different?' The goal of the counselor is to help the couple to live up to their contract with each other to behave differently. Anxiety will often rise and the counselor is tempted to process what is going on, but sticking with the task of the couple doing something differently is critical. Once something different is done the generation of additional options can be helpful. Sometimes couples can be coaxed into trying new behaviors by indicating that the session is really a laboratory in which they can experiment with new behavior. They do not need to get the behavior right the first time, they just need to try out some new behaviors.

The counselor may also instruct the couple to engage in some specific new behavior either in or out of the session. For example, if one member of the couple is particularly argumentative the counselor might ask them to lie on the floor during the discussion. Or requesting the couple to stop for a moment and breathe deeply may alter the mood enough that they are capable of relating, at least briefly, in a new way. These new experiences may produce an increased sense of freedom and hope.

To experience success is gratifying. Couples can be encouraged or directed to engage in self-chosen behaviors that have a high potential for success (Beavers & Kaslow, 1981). The 'self-chosen' aspect of the behavior is critical in terms of experiencing success. Behavior without personal involvement leads to hollow success. The behavior may be of either a couple or individual nature but if it is a couple activity both parties need to agree to engage in it.

Usually, a straightforward approach can be taken to planning.

The counselor might indicate that often couples start to feel better when they bring some new activity into their life. Some may set a personal goal and often that works better at least initially. Then, the partners might be asked if there is any new behavior that they would like to start as a couple. Reading, exercise, weight loss, etc. are often fulfilling behaviors that people choose. Engagement in the activity should be viewed as success. Failure to engage in a chosen activity does not need to be viewed as a failure experience. Rather the choosing of the goal can be viewed as an inappropriate choice at this time. The counselor might say to someone who had chosen to exercise but then not exercised, 'It doesn't seem that exercise is what you wanted to do, at least not now.'

Couples can also be directed to engage in new behaviors with each other in ways that ensure success.

Nathan and Mary had been seen for five sessions and the initial crisis in the relationship had been resolved. They had both committed to working on their marriage to see how good they could make it. The counselor in an effort to stimulate new caring behavior, while trying to provide the couple with optimal freedom and yet ensure the success of the intervention, gave the following directive,

Counselor: Nathan and Mary, this week I want you each on three occasions to express your love to the other person in a way that they understand. Often when we express love we do it in ways we would like to be loved, but I want you, Nathan, to focus on expressing your love to Mary in ways that she would appreciate and, Mary, I want you to do the same for Nathan. It is very possible, even likely, that your partner won't know what you have done. Next week, however, I'm going to ask each of you what you think the other did to express their love, but it's certainly okay if you're not sure what the other person was trying to do. Do you understand the instructions?

Almost always, if the couple are in a phase of counseling where they are moving closer together, this activity will be successful. It creates within each partner a focus, not on themselves, but on the other, 'Express your love in ways your partner will understand.' It also gives them freedom in choosing exactly what they want to do. The only failure is if they fail to engage in the task. Their agreement to participate can be secured before the homework is given. This 'blind commitment' to homework has been referred to as the 'devil's pact' (Watzlawick, Weakland, & Fisch, 1974) and is discussed in Chapter 6. It is the spirit of adventure, however, which can be created around the homework assignment that is often related to a renewal of hope.

Using a Community to Enrich the Relationship

A third path of action that can be hope-inducing for clients includes involvement in a personal community that enriches those aspects of their lives and relationship that they wish to nurture. At times this may mean redefining relationships and at other times it may mean forging new relationships. For instance, a young couple in a new community may benefit from establishing contacts with others who are also starting their relationship while an older couple, after retirement, may benefit from renewing old friendships.

The counselor can play two important roles in the couple's search for a healing and nurturing environment. First, she or he can assist with the evaluation and adjustment processes that couples must make relative to their social network. Secondly, the counselor can be an important referral source. She or he can help couples find the kind of formal and sometimes informal support systems they need to make progress in their relationship.

The social networks of clients have both supportive and interfering elements (Richardson, Barbour, & Bubenzer, 1991). Individuals, families, and groups may be supportive, interfering, or both. Couples benefit from evaluating their social networks in the light of their goal of building a successful, meaningful relationship. At times such an evaluation may mean giving up certain relationships, at other times it may mean making adjustments in relationships and, at still other times, it may mean becoming involved with new people. For example, it is not unusual to find a young married couple experiencing less interest in their single friends and more interest in spending time with others who have also been recently married. It seems that the common experience of living in and preparing for an intimate relationship can bond couples together and this bond can serve to inject hope and motivation into the relationship.

The counselor's role is primarily that of helping the couple to evaluate and make decisions about their social network. Facilitation of change and providing support as changes occur are also important functions of the counselor. The ultimate question that must be kept in front of the couple is, 'What do they need to do for the good of their relationship?' Such a question does not necessarily mean that the couple need more 'together' time and less individual time. However, once couples become committed to the marital goal it makes evaluation of the social network easier. Issues about friends, extended family, religious and social organization involvement, etc. can be more easily evaluated when the priority of the marriage is established.

Counselors also serve as referral sources for couples. Often the issues of a marriage extend beyond the realm of support that can be given in a counselor's office or even by a community of friends. Issues of substance abuse, physical and/or sexual abuse, and sometimes grief often require involvement with counseling groups for successful resolution. A major element of hope provided by a counseling group is the experience of mutuality (Yalom, 1985). Mutuality is an experience of affiliation characterized by caring, sharing, trust, and a feeling of belonging. It allows each spouse to know that what they are experiencing is not unique, but an experience shared by others. They also see that others have made it through their dilemmas and gone on to have successful marriages. Hopefully, when the group support can advance the therapeutic goals, counselors will take the lead in providing couples with referrals.

Summary

An important aspect of couples counseling lies in developing the couple's motivation and adaptive capacity. The concepts of hope and despair, fear and confidence, trust and mistrust are important in developing the flexibility and problem-solving skills necessary for a successful intimate relationship. Counselors have available a variety of communication, observation and reflection, and action tools to help couples experience life in a way that frees them from entrapment and helps them envision a hopeful future. This chapter has been used to review some of those tools.

5

Interventions to Address Issues of Comprehension

As previously mentioned, a couple often demonstrate patterns of relating that reflect rules for behaving. Although these patterns may have been repeated over a prolonged period of time, they remain outside the couple's level of awareness. Gaining an awareness of the patterns increases the couple's understanding of how problems are maintained in the relationship. That is, more than understanding the origin of problems or who is at fault in the relationship, we are attempting to comprehend patterns of interaction that help to maintain the presenting problem(s). For example, a couple expressed confusion and despair about continued conflict around 'insignificant' issues. Some relief was experienced as they began to see that they were embroiled in a symmetrical power struggle to define who was in charge of their relationship. Naturally, this power struggle was played out daily around any number of minor issues. Having a clear understanding of the patterns in their relationship that led to the escalation of conflict seemed to produce hope that the conflict could be reduced. Sometimes when the couple increase their comprehension of how presenting problems are maintained by patterns of interaction in the relationship, they are able to control their affect and engage in problem-solving efforts. Like Friedman (1990), we feel that couples experience more success in comprehending the systemic nature of their relationship when they are moving toward rather than away from the counselor. That is, comprehension or understanding interventions seem to have been most helpful in facilitating change when the couple have demonstrated an openness to new patterns of behavior. This openness may have been demonstrated while interacting in the counselor's office or after compliantly carrying out a number of homework assignments. The remainder of the chapter will focus on procedures used in couples counseling for helping partners comprehend the systemic or interactional nature of their relationship rather than viewing problems as simply residing in one member (see Figure 5.1).

Circular questioning focuses on gaining information about relationships rather than an individual.

Enactment means asking a couple to discuss some concern.

Reframing is redefining a problem from residing in an individual to residing in the relationship.

Relabeling is changing the label attached to a pattern of interaction from a negative to a positive label or vice versa.

Family choreography is physically sculpting or arranging partners in a manner that is descriptive of their relationship and then injecting movement into the sculpting to help it come alive.

Therapeutic reversals means the co-counselors role play the couple's pattern of interaction and, thus, place some distance between the couple and their pattern of interaction; as a result, the pattern is thought to be more easily comprehended.

Metaphorical stories are stories describing in symbolic ways patterns of interaction in the couple's relationship.

Genogram is a two- or three-generational picture of the family depicting historical patterns and forces outside the couple's relationship that impact on the relationship.

Describing observations is the counselor describing observable patterns of interaction in the couple's relationship.

Figure 5.1 *Interventions for helping the couple comprehend the systemic nature of their relationship*

Circular Questioning

While linear questioning is used within an intrapsychic model for finding out more about an individual (Tomm, 1988), circular questioning is used for gaining more information about relationships (Selvini Palazzoli et al., 1980). With linear questioning a counselor may ask the following: 'What has brought you to counseling?' 'When did you first notice this problem?' 'What have you noticed yourself doing to make the problem worse or better?' Obviously, these questions focus on learning more about the individual.

Madanes (1981) suggested we will notice rules for the couple's relationship being enacted as the couple negotiate a variety of issues: for example, leisure time, finances, sexual matters, contact with in-laws, and parenting. As an illustration, a child can develop a problem that draws the couple's attention away from their relationship and onto parenting, and Madanes suggested that we can notice patterns of interaction from the marital relationship being demonstrated around parenting concerns. As a result, circular questioning can be used when the counselor asks for the description of a relationship by some third party (Selvini Palazzoli et al., 1980). For instance, with a family where a child is presented as the identified client, we might ask the mother how the father responds to a child's problematic behavior and find that he is very involved and, from the mother's perspective, inappropriately involved. Then, the counselor might ask a sibling how the mother responds to the father's parenting efforts and how the father reacts to the mother's comments. The counselor might discover that the parents find themselves embroiled in conflict when the father initiates parenting. Likewise, when the father is asked how the mother responds to the child's behavior, the counselor might find that he also describes her as highly and inappropriately involved. Again, circular questioning could be extended even further by asking a sibling how the father responds to the mother's parenting efforts and how the mother reacts to the father's comments. It could occur that a symmetrical rule and pattern of interaction exists for parenting, where each thinks she or he knows the 'right' way to parent and criticizes the other, and this pattern may also be demonstrated around a variety of marital issues.

This same approach to circular questioning, having a third person describe a dyadic relationship, might also be used when working with the couple and extended members from the family of origin. Here, the counselor might ask a partner as well as extended members to describe each spouse's relationship with the family. For instance, 'What has been your wife's response to your father's illness?' 'How has your mother responded to your wife's efforts to be helpful?' 'How has your husband reacted to his father's illness?' 'How has your mother-in-law reacted to your husband's level of concern for his father?' 'Who has been most involved with your husband's illness, your daughter-in-law or your son?' The counselor may learn that the wife is very responsible and active in taking care of the husband's aging father while the husband is rather disengaged from the entire process. It may occur that this complementary rule and pattern of interaction, with one partner being more dominant or responsible and the other being more disengaged, is also demonstrated as the couple negotiate other issues in their relationship. As the counselor gains increased understanding of the couple's relationship, the couple also gain increased comprehension of the rules and patterns of interaction in their relationship.

Enactment

Besides the use of circular questioning, enactments (Minuchin & Fishman, 1981) can be used to increase the counselor and couple's understanding of problematic patterns of interaction. An enactment is used when the counselor asks the couple to talk with each other and come to some conclusion about the nature of their problem or how it might be resolved. Minuchin and Fishman noted three steps in creating an enactment: (a) observe some spontaneous transaction between the couple then decide on a concern to be highlighted; (b) organize a scenario in which the couple are directed to discuss their concern; and (c) once the couple slide into redundant and nonproductive patterns of interaction, suggest an alternative way of transacting.

> A couple enter counseling with concern for the husband's depression. They both tell the counselor about the onset of the depression after an industrial accident. The husband experienced a slipped disk from the accident that prevented him from lifting heavy objects and resulted in the loss of his job. This occurred a year ago and although he had been able to drive the car, get himself around town and do many things for himself, he frequently remained home during the day in his bath robe with little energy to leave the house. The wife worked as a nurse and took care of the husband's needs when she was home. When the counselor directed the couple to discuss what needed to be done to relieve the husband's depression, a pattern developed where the wife told the husband how he needed to help with chores around the house and get busy looking for a new job. During this enactment the husband offered minimal responses to his wife's suggestions and took on the role of a passive listener with little willingness to generate ideas on how to relieve his depression.

> *Counselor*: I'd like the two of you to talk about what you think needs to be done to help Bob get over his depression.
> *Wife*: Well, I've told you that you'd feel much better if only you'd get out of that old bath robe and get busy.
> *Husband*: Yea, I know.
> *Wife*: I know I always feel better when I'm productive. I'm sure if you'd pick up the newspaper and turn to the classified section you'd find many jobs.
> *Husband*: I suppose.
> *Wife*: And until you find a job there are many chores around

the house that need to be done. You know those windows
need caulking and the leak in the basement needs to be fixed.
Husband: [*Sits quietly*]
Wife: [*talking to counselor*] See, this is how it always goes.
He'd feel much better if he'd only listen to me.

In the above enactment the counselor may have suggested an
alternative way of interacting and asked the husband to tell the
wife what he thought needed to be done to relieve his depression.
More than likely, however, the couple would have been unable to
respond to this alternative and the wife would have moved back
into providing suggestions and the husband would have reverted
into a passive listener. By creating this enactment, by extending it
beyond the point where the couple would usually have stopped
talking with one another, and by offering alternative ways for
discussing the problem, the counselor may have been able to
observe and learn about the couple's pattern and rules for relating.
The couple could have also begun to experience and comprehend
that, in part, the husband's depression was maintained by patterns
of interaction in their relationship. Again, the depression could
have been viewed as not just the husband's problem but a relationship problem. Of course, enactments like this may occur spon-
taneously and may not need to be created. The wife may have
given the husband suggestions about overcoming his depression
while the husband passively listened and, then, the counselor could
have followed up with directives for alternative ways of having the
couple discuss the husband's depression. The point is that the
enactment gives the counselor an opportunity to observe patterns
of interaction in the relationship and, by directing the couple to
extend the enactment beyond the point where they would usually
stop interacting, the counselor provides the couple with an opportunity to experience and comprehend how these patterns contribute
to the presenting problem.

Reframing and Relabeling

Like circular questioning and enactments, reframing helps the
couple understand the systemic patterns of interaction in their relationship. With reframing, the meaning attributed to a situation is
changed and the definition of the problem is changed from residing
within one member of the relationship to a definition that
attributes the problem as belonging to the relationship (Selvini
Palazzoli et al., 1978; Weeks & L'Abate, 1982). Relabeling refers
to changing the label attached to a person or problem without

necessarily moving from an individual to a systemic level; for instance, an undesirable behavior may receive a positive label (withdrawing described as contemplating) or a desirable behavior may receive a negative label (interest in others described as over-involvement) (Weeks & L'Abate, 1982). Since there are multiple ways to comprehend couples and their problems, the point to remember is that we want to reframe and relabel in a way that can help the couple comprehend the presenting problem as residing in their relationship.

As has been noted by Weeks and L'Abate, we often view reframing and relabeling as overlapping techniques. That is, in providing an undesirable behavior with a positive label (or vice versa) we also usually move the context of the problem from an intrapsychic level to a systems level. For instance, in a symmetrical relationship where each partner accuses the other of being unfeeling, critical and the cause of the marital problem, the counselor may help the couple comprehend the systemic nature of their presenting complaint by reframing and relabeling the criticism as the vehicle for maintaining closeness in the relationship. Or, a couple may be stuck in a complementary pattern, where the presenting problem revolves around a wife who often finds herself overcommitted to a variety of promises she has made to others and complaining that the husband never wants to help her meet social obligations. When they do get together with others the husband often seems uncomfortable, withdrawn, and the wife complains that her enjoyment is limited by needing to look after the husband. Here, the counselor might help the couple comprehend the systemic nature of their presenting concern by reframing and relabeling the husband's social avoidance as functioning like the governor on an engine and slowing down the number of obligations to which the wife is committed.

Since there is no one way to comprehend couples and their problems, the point for the counselor to remember is to frame and label problems in a way that increases the leverage for change. The couple's comprehension of their problem at the time they enter counseling is one of the main reasons they remain stuck in non-productive patterns of behavior. Reframing and relabeling of the presenting problems helps the couple change their phenomenological perspective and provides the couple with a new way of thinking about their relationship (Weeks & L'Abate, 1982).

Family Choreography

Family choreography can be viewed as an extension of family sculpting. Sculpting occurs when the counselor provides each member of the relationship with an opportunity to physically arrange himself or herself and partner in such a manner as to represent their relationship at a particular moment in time (Simon, 1972). While sculpting is more of a static description of the relationship, choreography would attempt to capture the fluidness of the relationship (Papp, 1976). With choreography the counselor has each partner place their mate and themselves in a position that is descriptive of the relationship. The partner who is choreographing the relationship is also helped to decide what movement needs to be included to make the positioning come alive. As an illustration, one partner attempting to differentiate from the family of origin may choreograph the couple's relationship with one of her hands tied to pieces of furniture (representing the family of origin) and the other hand grasping her partner. Life is then injected into the scene as the choreographer describes how she feels pulled between the partner and the demands from the parents. The choreographer may begin to sway and move first in the direction of the partner and then in her family of origin's direction to physically represent pulls within the system.

Because the couple are helped to see and physically experience patterns of interacting, choreography may be used to help transcend language (Papp, 1976) and, as a result, the couple may be in a better position to comprehend the reciprocity in their relationship. We often find it helpful to initiate the choreography by showing the couple how their relationship appears to us. For example, with one type of dominant–submissive relationship, the counselor might direct the dominant partner to stand and the submissive partner to kneel. A leash may be attached between the partners and whichever one is standing may be instructed to lead the other around the room. Each member needs to be provided with an opportunity to choreograph the relationship as she or he sees it. As with sculpting (Simon, 1972), the incongruities between the partners' views of the relationship may be more accessible through choreographing. It is our experience, however, that the counselor's choreography is often most helpful and often recognized by the couple as being an accurate view of their relationship. After choreographing how the relationship is, the couple may be able to choreograph their ideal relationship and talk about how to move in the ideal direction. Comprehension can be facilitated by asking each to describe their choreography as it is being developed. Again, this procedure is designed to broaden the couple's comprehension of the relationship beyond that of a linear model where one person is viewed as the cause of the couple's problems and the other as the recipient of the guilty partner's behavior.

Therapeutic Reversals

Like choreography, reversals can be used to transcend the couple's description of their complaints about one another and to help them comprehend the reciprocity of the relationship. Two types of reversals can be used in couples counseling. In the first instance the couple might simply be asked to reverse roles: to assume the body posture, mannerisms, attitude, and verbalizations of their partner. The counselor might interview the partners when they are in the role-reversed position to see what they understand their partner to be thinking or feeling. This partner reversal accomplishes three objectives. First, it allows the counselor to assess the level of comprehension each spouse has about their partner. In the interview portion of the role play the counselor can see whether or not the partners can remove themselves enough from the struggle to understand their partner and the way the two of them work together to maintain their problem. Second, the role-reversal process sometimes allows the couple to grow in their understanding of their relationship. By taking an 'insider's view' of what the partner experiences in the relationship the couple deepen their understanding of the relationship. Finally, if the couple are asked to solve their problems from their reversed role positions, new perspectives and solutions are sometimes generated.

In our second instance of the use of therapeutic reversals within couples counseling, the couple can be asked to exchange roles with the counselor(s). We view this reversal as an example of what Barker (1985) terms a relationship metaphor, where one relationship (the co-counselors' relationship) becomes a metaphor for the couple's relationship. This technique has proven to be most helpful when there is a therapeutic impasse in helping the couple to change. If co-counselors are working with the couple and if they are exhausted in their efforts to bring about change with the couple, it is sometimes helpful for the couple and the counselors to exchange roles. The counselors now play the couple in a way similar to how the couple behave in the session and the couple are asked to be helpful to them. After a few minutes of playing these reversed roles the counselors return to their roles and the couple again assume the client role. Frequently, the couple will have new insight into their relationship and the counselors will have new ideas about the direction that can be taken in counseling. Even if there is a single counselor, she or he can exchange roles with either partner and the displaced individual will gain an 'outsider's' view of the relationship. Such a view will usually contain some new ideas about the relationship and about the role one plays in either maintaining the problem or in bringing about solutions. It is assumed that being able to sit back and watch the counselors role-play the couple places some distance between the couple and their patterns of interaction; thus, the patterns are thought to be more easily comprehended.

Metaphorical Stories

A couple in their late thirties entered counseling after having been married for a few years. In this complementary relationship the wife had taken the dominant role by making sure that household duties were met, paying bills, cooking meals, cleaning, accomplishing home maintenance, etc. The husband was heavily involved in his career and a large portion of his free time was spent working out with 'boys' from the office. The crisis in the relationship occurred when the wife became pregnant and was confined to bed and could no longer fulfill the household responsibilities. The husband became embittered with the new expectations of him at home and the wife resented his unwillingness to become more active at home during the pregnancy. The pregnancy reached termination and a healthy son was born but, in the year following the birth and preceding entry into counseling, the couple were engulfed in conflict as both felt abused and not appreciated in the relationship.

It was during this time that the husband had become friends with a female coworker from his office and, while he reported that they had not been sexually involved, he described her as providing understanding and support during this difficult period in his marriage. Although this relationship had ended by the time they entered couples counseling, the wife reported being angry and hurt by this relationship, and she felt it had driven the two of them further apart. The couple had been in counseling for about three months, and while the husband was making some effort to become more involved at home, he at times still appeared to resent the new expectations. The wife, at times, also expressed irritation at his resentment as well as unresolved anger around the husband's relationship with the coworker. To some extent, each still seemed to view problems in the relationship as residing in their partner and the pain of the affair was still quite evident in the relationship. During the seventh session the following metaphor was delivered:

We sat for some time yesterday after your session and we were touched by all that you have experienced in recent years. It seems as though you have been caught in one of those lengthy storms, where nightfall sets in and there is an eerie quietness of both impending excitement and also a feeling of apprehension. Each of you do your part to see that you will be prepared when the storm hits. You lay out candles, unplug the radios and one of the TVs, find the flashlight, and talk a bit about going to the basement if the storm really is bad. All evening you both watch TV and notice that the 'W' stays in the upper left hand corner and read the words that move along the bottom of the screen warning of the approaching storm. You both do your job and don't say much to each other, being careful not to heighten your own fears or the fear of each other. You retire, but are restless.

After a while the wind begins to rise and you see flashes of lightning and hear the rain hit the windows. You rise to close the windows, calm the dog, make sure the freezer is working. You hear the lightning hit the phone wires and remember to unplug the other TV. At the same time, you now feel cut off from the outside world not knowing what is going on around you or when the storm will pass. Finally, the wind eases and you both return to bed but still sleep fitfully.

Soon after, you hear the wind rise again and you hear the storm warning sirens droning faintly in the distance. You both get up again to face the new storm. You start in different directions to check windows and doors. The storm worsens and you hear the crash of a tree on the house. You are separated and one of you decides to head for the basement while the other heads for the door fearing the house will catch on fire from the fallen tree. You are both looking for each other with arms extended, reaching out to feel the strength and security that is needed. One of you touches and finds some of the caring, concern and understanding needed to get you through the night. The two huddle down waiting for the storm to end. When morning dawns, and you can begin to see again, the one of you who made contact and found some of the encouragement and understanding that was needed to make it through the night realizes they are not with their spouse. They feel anxious about this and yet they are grateful for having someone to help them through the storm. The dawning of the new day leaves the other feeling lonely, abandoned, angry and frightened about where their spouse disappeared to in the night.

As the day grows brighter and clearer, you stumble onto each other again. The reunion is filled with apprehension, 'Where were you when the storm really hit?' 'When will the next storm hit?' 'Will you be there when it comes again?' There is also that issue of saying good-bye to the one who was there during the dark of the night. You realize that the two of you can forecast and to some extent control the weather and that this is exciting and frightening given the extent of the previous storms.

In this story, an effort was made to explain the function of the unresolved problem (the relationship with the coworker) in the couple's relationship. This seemed to place the husband's relationship with the coworker in the context of the marriage rather than explaining the relationship as simply involving the husband and excluding the wife.

Metaphorical stories like this one are used to help the couple comprehend a similarity between their relationship and persons or objects in the story. As with other interventions mentioned in this chapter, story telling allows for some emotional distance as the couple look at a symbolic representation of their relationship. This indirect experiencing of their relationship can facilitate an alteration in the couple's perceptual predisposition and, thus, move the couple to a place where they view conflict as a relationship rather than individual problem. It should be mentioned that in creating a metaphorical story the counselor needs to obtain an understanding of the systemic dynamics in the couple's relationship (such as, hierarchy, subsystem boundaries, changes in the life cycle, reciprocal patterns of interaction, etc.). Then characters are built into the story to represent the couple and the story is developed around those dynamics that keep them stuck in an unsatisfactory relationship. The story in this section focused on how the couple's relationship had moved to a triadic unit (including a coworker) when stress and tension were experienced and, so, it was suggested that problems can be viewed as being broader based than simply residing in one partner.

It has also been our experience that the delivery of the story is critical to its success, and this usually requires preparation and practice prior to the couple's counseling session. For instance, counselors occasionally wonder how to introduce a metaphorical story to the couple. If the counselor wants to introduce a story at the beginning of a session, it may be enough to say 'You know, during this past week an interesting story came to my mind.' If after delivering the story the couple comment on a connection between their relationship and the story, the counselor might simply attribute the connection to client insight and ask the couple to elaborate on the connection. Obviously, the couple do not need to discuss the connection between the story and their relationship. If, however, the couple do not even comment on the story, the counselor might ask 'What did you think of that story?' or 'Could you have thought of a different ending to that story?'

Barker (1985) has also included thought on distinguishing good from poor story telling. For example, he suggested that counselors should take their time and not rush through the story and that counselors might want to mark what the story is trying to emphasize with procedures like slowing down the delivery at significant moments. Indeed, it would appear that counselors wanting to use metaphorical stories in couples counseling could benefit from time spent in preparing the story and practicing its delivery.

Genograms

We have found that genograms are best constructed with a blackboard and chalk or easel and felt marker after the counselor has some idea of the couple's presenting problem. In couples counseling the genogram is at least a two-generational description of the family and, if the couple have children, a three-generational description can be developed. The genogram is used as a convenient device for helping the counselor gather a large amount of information about the couple and for helping the couple comprehend historical and current influences from the larger family context on their present relationship (McGoldrick & Gerson, 1985). Specifically, the genogram can be used to show how patterns in one generation repeat themselves in the next generation, to illustrate the symmetrical or complementary nature of the couple's relationship, to show the rigid or diffuse boundaries between the couple's subsystem and those outside their relationship, and to describe the pattern of interaction that keeps other people or activities triangled into their relationship. In creating a genogram counselors can use symbols suggested by Guerin and Pendagast (1976) and McGoldrick and Gerson (1985) to represent family members and relationships among members (see Figure 5.2).

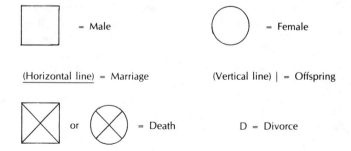

Figure 5.2 *Genogram symbols*

The genogram in Figure 5.3 was constructed for Rocky and Camille, a couple in the first year of their marriage. The presenting problem was that Rocky and Camille found themselves with minor disagreements that escalated into larger conflicts. Indeed, during the session small disagreements stemming from issues like being late for appointments were escalated as Rocky challenged Camille and gradually became louder and more accusatory and as Camille became quiet and withdrew. They also cited examples of other couples having asked them out and, on occasion, at the last minute Camille would be unable to go and Rocky would explode and say that she should have notified him earlier. Of course, Camille had not wished to go out on these occasions but felt uneasy about saying so to Rocky.

The genogram indicates that the couple were married in 1988, reside in Chicago, and do not have any children. Rocky is the older of two, with a brother who was recently divorced and is living in Springfield with his parents. Camille was the younger of two with an older brother who lives in Denver with his wife. Camille's parents were married in 1958 and live in Chicago.

In asking the couple about their contact with extended family members, it was discovered that Camille and her mother were quite close, calling on the telephone every other day, and Rocky and Camille often had Sunday supper at her parents' home. The couple mentioned wanting to create some distance between themselves and Camille's parents but struggled with this since they perceived Camille as her mother's best friend.

Both were asked to describe their parents' relationships when they were growing up and each remembered their father as a 'yeller.' Rocky remembered his mother as quiet and withdrawn, and Camille recalled her mother as quiet and working hard to please her father. It was easy to draw connections between Rocky and Camille's style of negotiating differences and that of their parents, with Rocky confronting and Camille withdrawing, and the more Rocky confronted the more Camille withdrew, and the more she withdrew the more Rocky confronted. The couple became even more unsettled with this complementary style of negotiation when the counselor suggested that it may be a way of hanging on to their parents and they may want to think twice before giving it up.

While the genogram is a handy way of gathering information about the couple's relationship, visualizing the genogram on a blackboard

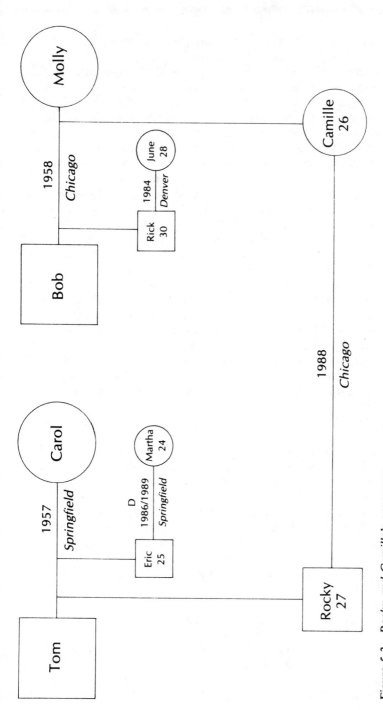

Figure 5.3 *Rocky and Camille's genogram*

or easel seems to also help the couple comprehend their relationship as part of a larger family context.

Initially, the genogram is merely a skeleton of two or three family generations, and the counselor relies on appropriate questioning to flesh out the skeleton. For instance, we would usually develop a genogram after knowing something about the couple's presenting problem and patterns of interaction in their relationship. Then the counselor could explore multigenerational patterns of interaction by, for example, asking, 'How would you describe your parents' relationship?' 'What issues were they in conflict over?' 'How did they handle differences?' 'What was their approach to parenting?' 'How did they divide work and various other responsibilities?' and 'How did they support each other?' Or, if the couple report chronic financial distress, they might be asked who else in the family has also experienced financial difficulty. The couple might also be asked to comment on how other members of their family had handled financial distress and if that resembled problem solving used in their own relationship. Problem areas outlined in Chapter 1 can all be traced through genograms. The counselor will also want to find out if the couple's current interaction with extended family members is impacting on their relationship and might ask questions like, 'Who else in your family is aware of the concerns in your relationship?' 'What have they done or said to try to be helpful to you?' 'How do you regard and respond to their involvement in your lives?' 'How have these folks responded to your reactions concerning their involvement in your lives?'

The focus of genograming is to develop a skeleton map of the couple's multigenerational context and to fill out the map with questions and supportive statements. Drawing the genogram on a blackboard or easel seems to place some distance between the couple and their patterns of interacting and, thus, appears to facilitate comprehension. During this process, the counselor is continually listening for repeated patterns and, as patterns are observed, the counselor may share observations with the couple to increase their comprehension of the systemic dynamics in their relationship.

Describing Observations

Finally, Umbarger (1983) suggested that counselors can help couples comprehend the systemic nature of their relationship by describing the roles each plays as they interact. Here, the counselor is describing the observable behaviors each demonstrates as they interact with each other. This differs from an interpretation which relies on an intrapsychic rather than interpersonal perspective. That is, interpretations are a description of the motivations and meanings behind a client's behavior while systemic descriptions of patterns of interaction highlight the observable behaviors of each member of the relationship. For instance, an interpretation might indicate 'Your anger at Tom seems to be masking a great deal of unresolved disappointment' whereas a behavioral observation of a pattern in the couple's relationship might indicate that 'When Tom declines the invitation to get involved with Jane, Jane seems to become angry and Tom responds by withdrawing further, which seems to fuel Jane's anger, until both eventually fall into silence.' Umbarger noted, 'a successful description requires the therapist to assess the mood of the family [couple], timing, who is to be included in the description, and so forth; when the system is attentive and open to new information, then a sequence description can be most helpful' (1983: 137).

As was previously suggested, efforts to increase the couple's systemic understanding of their relationship seem most fruitful when the couple are moving toward rather than away from the counselor (Friedman, 1990). That is, when they have demonstrated an openness to alternative patterns of behavior while interacting in the counselor's office or after compliantly carrying out homework assignments. Indeed, before attempting to increase the couple's systemic understanding of their relationship, the counselor wants to consider their receptiveness to this information. Because, of course, making a correct observation is of little importance if the effect has not been to increase systemic understanding.

Minuchin and Fishman also described an approach for delivering a behavioral observation that is designed to increase the couple's comprehension of the systemic nature of their relationship. They suggested that the counselor describe the behavior of one member and then assign responsibility for that behavior to the other member. One of their illustrations reads as follows, 'Your wife seems to control all the decisions in this family. How did you engineer all of that work for her?' (1981: 197). Another illustration could read, 'Your husband does seem to have a problem controlling his emotions. In what ways have you become the more reasonable or thoughtful side of his life?' The point here is that by describing an observable and unacceptable behavior and by then assigning some of the responsibility for the behavior to the other partner, the counselor is helping the couple develop a broader, more systemic understanding of their relationship. Again, it is the systemic perspective that helps each partner to realize that, 'This relationship is, in part, based on my behavior.'

Summary

Each of the therapeutic interventions presented in this chapter is designed, in part, to help the couple further comprehend the systemic nature of their relationship. Again, we would believe that some of what keeps the couple stuck in nonproductive patterns of interaction can be attributed to how they understand and view their concerns; that is, viewing the presenting problem as simply residing in one of the two partners. We have thought it to be more helpful if the couple can understand the presenting problem as a function of the relationship.

We do want to note that there are instances in which the promotion of an individual view as well as a systemic view of problems may be crucial. Although we do think that systemic aspects of couple relationships support the maintenance of problems, we are aware that there are problems that individuals have that also deserve attention independent of the couple relationship, such as alcoholism. Therefore, we do not think it is always helpful to promote only a systemic view of problems. At times there are issues of such dangerous potential – substance abuse, physical and sexual abuse, threats of suicide and homicide, etc. – that the counselor's first concern has to be the safety of all parties. Usually, the providing of support and urging and sometimes requiring of individual treatment for both the 'perpetrator' and 'victim' is an appropriate step. A systemic perspective of the couple relationship will be reintroduced once the addictive or dangerous behavior has been eliminated or significantly reduced. We do think the control of dangerous behavior in the relationship should always be a high priority.

The interventions presented in this chapter are only a representation of the procedures that can be used to help the couple develop a better understanding of their relationship and the function of the presenting problem in the relationship. The reader is encouraged to consider other means for increasing client comprehension.

6
Managing In-Session Behaviour

Any system requires some behavioral management skills in order to operate efficiently and this also holds for the couples counseling system that includes the counselor and the couple. The counselor's ability to implement behavioral management skills during the counseling session is usually summoned when one or both partners stop listening, fail to work at understanding one another and, instead, fall into accustomed and problematic patterns of interaction. These patterns often resemble the previously defined complementary and symmetrical styles (see Figure 2.3) and numerous illustrations of each can be observed.

Complementary and Symmetrical Styles

Lederer and Jackson thought of the complementary relationship as 'one in which (at the extreme) one spouse is in charge and the other obeys' (1968: 161). An understanding of complementarity suggests that it occurs when one partner complements or in some way completes behavior of the other, so, for example, one partner may become demanding while the other becomes pleasing, or one may become incompetent and childlike while the other becomes competent and parental, or one may become physically or psychologically troubled while the other appears healthy and in good spirits. In contrast, it is also possible for one partner to be 'in charge' of certain tasks in the relationship while the mate assumes responsibility for additional duties, and this might promote a very satisfactory relationship. For indeed, some accommodation and sharing of responsibility is required in any successful relationship. It is when one partner is always in charge of decisions, is always demanding, competent, or healthy and the other is always obeying, pleasing, incompetent, or troubled that the power or influence in the relationship is out of balance. It is during these periods that couples present themselves for counseling and, when these patterns of interaction are enacted in the counselor's office, behavior management procedures can be used to challenge the rigidly maintained patterns. Challenging the rigidly maintained pattern also momentarily helps the couple beyond the therapeutic impasse.

Lederer and Jackson noted that in the symmetrical relationship each partner is continually stating through behavior that, 'I am as good as you are' (1968: 161). During the counseling session these couples can be noticed demonstrating competence by working at taking charge, by making demands of each other, or by finding fault with one another. A broader definition of symmetry suggests that it refers to similarity in form or arrangement. Here, we might also think of a couple in which each partner exhibits childlike competence. In this case the similarity in form or arrangement is displayed through incompetence. On the other hand, a couple might also agree that either partner can effectively complete a particular task and, consequently, even assist each other with chores but not reach the point where either is trying to control the relationship. In this case, an egalitarian relationship exists without the destructive competitiveness that aims to control the relationship.

When symmetrical relationships do escalate into destructive power struggles, couples often present themselves in the counselor's office with each demanding that the other somehow change. When these destructive symmetrical patterns surface during the course of counseling, the counselor must be able to use behavioral management procedures to challenge the symmetrically escalating power struggle and to reintroduce an element of complementarity back into the relationship. While it is the intent of some interventions to increase the couple's systemic comprehension of their relationship (see Chapter 5), it is the purpose of the behavioral management interventions to challenge the couple's patterns of behavior and this chapter considers behavioral management interventions that can be used during the session.

Destabilizing Old Patterns of Interaction

Behavioral management procedures are used in a counseling session at the moment when the couple are repeating a pattern of interaction that they have frequently demonstrated and that keeps them stuck in an unsatisfactory relationship. Complementary and symmetrical relationships may call for different approaches.

Destabilizing Complementary Patterns
Consider the example of Mo and Alastair.

Mo: We can't go on like this. I keep wanting us to go out and do things with other people and you continue to feel uncomfortable with socializing. So either we go out and I worry about you having a bad time or we stay home.

Alastair: You're right. It seems that I can't think of anything to say when we're with other people.

Mo: I can't understand that. You need to be more like me. Just relax and tell people about the things you're doing or appear to be interested in their families and jobs. That is what everyone else does.

Alastair: I'm just not at ease in a group of people.

Mo: Well, we both know that growing up in the country didn't give you a lot of practice at being sociable. Let's go out this weekend and plan to have you stay close to me so you can become part of the conversations I initiate.

Alastair: We could try that.

In-session behavioral management interventions attempt to destabilize accustomed patterns like those cited in the example of Mo and Alastair. Interventions that may be helpful in destabilizing a complementary relationship include the counselor (a) becoming an alter ego, (b) asking, 'What would it be like to be married to me?' (c) using a stop watch to control talk time, (d) supporting the more submissive partner, and (e) demonstrating boredom with the complementary pattern (see Figure 6.1). Each of these in-session behavioral management interventions will now be briefly described.

Becoming an alter ego   is interrupting a complementary pattern by helping each partner identify unexpressed thoughts and feelings that may move the couple's interaction to a level where they can discuss the consequences of their complementary style.

Asking 'What would it be like to be married to me?'   is an effort to bring the complementary pattern to a halt, to explore the consequences of the complementary style, and to help each partner look at their contribution to the complementary pattern.

Using a stop watch to control talk time   is an effort to break up a complementary pattern where one partner dominates talk time.

Supporting the more submissive partner   is forming a momentary alliance with the more submissive partner and helping him or her become more assertive in the relationship, and, thereby, destabilizing the complementary pattern.

Demonstrating boredom with a complementary pattern   means demonstrating boredom when the couple resort to their complementary pattern of interaction.

Figure 6.1   *Interventions for destabilizing a complementary relationship*

Becoming an Alter Ego. One way to interrupt nonproductive behavioral patterns in a couple's relationship is for the counselor to become the alter ego for each partner (Piercy, 1991). In order to use this intervention with a couple, the counselor might simply say 'stop' when one partner becomes involved in a lecturette or monologue and when the other passively listens. Then the counselor can position chairs to the side and slightly behind each partner and explain that she or he is going to help each express thoughts and feelings as they occur. As the couple begin to interact and as the complementary pattern surfaces, the counselor might slip into the chair next to the dominant partner. Simply touching this partner's shoulder might interrupt the interaction and the counselor can say something like 'I'm certainly feeling ineffective and alone right now. I wonder if Alastair is really committed to supporting me in developing a friendship network and social life.'

Of course, the counselor will want to become the alter ego of both partners and, so, will no doubt need to be moving between the two chairs and sitting next to each mate several times. When sitting next to the more submissive partner, the counselor might hold up a hand indicating for the dominant partner to stop her or his monologue. Again, in a lower voice, the counselor might comment that 'I certainly feel like I've heard Mo's feelings before. I know I need to be doing something different but it's so much easier to just let her take the lead in social situations.' Use of the counselor as each partner's alter ego is a behavioral management intervention designed to interrupt a redundant complementary pattern during the counseling session and may have the effect of moving the couple's interaction to a level where they can now discuss the consequences of their complementary style. For instance, Mo and Alastair might be instructed to discuss the consequences of Mo feeling responsible for Alastair having a good time when out with friends.

Asking, 'What would it be Like to be Married to Someone Like Me?' This intervention is designed to help each partner look at their contribution to the complementary pattern (Piercy, 1991). First, however, by directing the couple to 'stop' as they slide into their accustomed pattern and by having them consider this question, the counselor brings a halt to the complementary style.

> *Counselor*: I'd like us to stop here for a moment, and I'd like you both to consider the following question, 'What would it be like to be married to someone like me?' I've brought paper and pencils and want you to separately consider your responses

for a moment and then write an answer to this question. After you've written your answers we'll discuss them.

As with the counselor becoming each partner's alter ego, the couple may now find themselves exploring the consequences of their complementary style of interaction. For instance, they might realize that with Alastair behaving like a social wallflower and with Mo worrying about his social competence the couple actually reduce the opportunity for a more egalitarian relationship. Most important, however, the counselor can use the procedure as a behavioral management intervention to interrupt the couple's continued expression of their complementary pattern of inter-action.

Using a Stop Watch to Control Talk Time.   The counselor may use a stop watch to break up the complementary pattern where one partner dominates the talk time. Here, the counselor instructs the couple to reach a resolution on some topic that is of concern. A stop watch is placed between them and they are told that whoever wants to talk must set the watch for 60 seconds and make their points within that time frame. Then, the watch is passed on to the other partner who in turn sets it for 60 seconds and has that period in which to respond. If one partner has nothing to say, they still set the stop watch for 60 seconds, hold it for that period of time and, then, pass it back to their mate. As an example, let us consider what the counselor might say to Mo and Alastair.

> *Counselor*: I brought this stop watch and I'm going to place it in front of you. I'd like one of you to pick up the watch and give yourself 60 seconds in which to tell the other how you'd like to handle your social life. When your 60 seconds is up, give the watch to your partner and she or he has 60 seconds to respond to your comments or share her or his thoughts about the two of you developing a social life. Even if you run out of things to say before your time is up, hold on to the watch for 60 seconds. I'd like you to continue passing the watch back and forth for the next 10 minutes. So, whoever wants to start, pick up the watch.

This intervention can have the effect of interrupting the monologues that are sometimes associated with complementary relationships and, secondarily, it can facilitate an awareness on the part of each partner that it is their dominant–submissive style that has become problematic to the relationship.

Supporting the More Submissive Partner. With this intervention the counselor might ask the more submissive partner to elaborate on those aspects of the relationship that are displeasing or disturbing to her or him. This intervention may be particularly appropriate when the submissive partner has historically been involved in 'pleasing' the dominant partner. The submissive partner may be urged to become more assertive in the relationship and momentarily destabilize the old complementary pattern. The counselor might strengthen this intervention by sitting closer to the more submissive partner and coaching her or him in making assertive statements about what they want from the relationship. This challenge to the relationship's organization might also need to be supported by the counselor blocking efforts on the part of the dominant partner to interrupt her or his more submissive mate. As Minuchin and Fishman (1981) suggested, when unbalancing a relationship the counselor wants to be aware of the impact of this intervention on the relationship. That is, while the counselor might momentarily form an alliance with the more submissive mate, later she or he will want to join with and be supportive of the other partner.

Again, let us consider Mo and Alastair's efforts to negotiate how they will handle social engagements. While Alastair probably would not be described as pleasing Mo, the following might be an illustration of the counselor bringing a complementary pattern to a halt by developing an alliance with the less dominant partner.

Counselor: Alastair, I hear you saying that you're receptive to Mo taking the lead and becoming part of the conversations she initiates, but I'm wondering if that will really occur.

Alastair: I don't know. Usually when we go out it's with friends from her school and, since I'm not familiar with their school-related issues, I often become rather quiet and withdrawn.

Counselor: Do the two of you spend time with other folks?

Alastair: We usually go out with couples from Mo's school.

Mo: If it wasn't for my friends we'd never go out.

Counselor: Hold on a minute, let's see where Alastair is on this issue. [*Counselor moves her or his chair closer to Alastair.*] What would you think about setting up an evening with a couple from your office or neighborhood? Perhaps a show, ball game, or something you'd enjoy?

Alastair: I think I could arrange that.

Counselor: Well let's say that you did, and let's say that you and Mo went out with one of these couples, what would you find to talk about?

Alastair: Oh, there are a few movies I've been wanting to see, and I can imagine going somewhere after a show and talking about the movie. I've also always liked baseball and if we went to a game I could certainly carry on a discussion about baseball.

Counselor: Is there something here that you'd be willing to do?

Alastair: Sure. I'd be willing to ask one of the fellows at work if he and his wife would want to join Mo and me for dinner and then go to a game.

As the counselor works at destabilizing a rigidly maintained pattern of interaction, she or he will want to continually side with one partner and then the other, thereby retaining a systemic perspective on the relationship. Without the ability to form alliances with both partners the counselor is at risk of seeing only one mate as the key to the couple's distress.

Demonstrating Boredom with a Complementary Pattern. When the couple resort to their complementary pattern of interacting and style of problem solving, the counselor may demonstrate boredom. For example, in an over-responsible–under-responsible relationship the over-responsible partner may continue to criticize her or his mate for forgetting responsibilities while the mate quietly listens and only occasionally provides an 'okay,' 'hum-hum,' or 'yup' response. This pattern may have demonstrated itself numerous times before and, as a result, the counselor may decide to show her or his boredom with the unproductive pattern by beginning to read a conveniently placed newspaper as the couple slip into their routine. Chances are that this redundant pattern will be brought to a screeching halt with the counselor's demonstration of boredom, and it is at this moment that the counselor may help the couple consider an alternative style of interacting for resolving grievances.

Destabilizing Symmetrical Patterns

Again, the reason for using in-session behavioral management interventions is that the traditional and nonproductive patterns of interaction may need to be destabilized before the couple become receptive to alternative styles of interacting. Of course, procedures also exist for destabilizing symmetrical styles of interacting. Let us consider the example of Sharon and Tom's symmetrical relationship.

Sharon: You know, Tom, we really need to spend time with my family this weekend. Last Saturday we were at your folks'.

Tom: Yea, but we never do anything once we get there but sit in the living room and visit. We could get so much more done by staying home.

Sharon: That's just like you. I give up one of my weekends to do what you want, but when I make a request you're too busy.

Tom: That's not true. What about the neighborhood picnic we went to two weeks ago? That certainly wasn't my idea of how to spend a Sunday.

Sharon: Are you saying you didn't have a good time? Then how was it that you spent the entire time with your friends instead of being with me?

Tom: I'm saying that we have a lot to do around the house and this isn't a good time to visit your parents.

With Sharon and Tom the counselor might destabilize their symmetrical relationship by (a) triangling herself or himself into their arguments or by creating physical distance between them, (b) by keeping score or by having payment made for critical comments, (c) by using a paradoxical intervention as a behavioral management intervention, (d) by remembering occasions that were exceptions to escalating conflict, and (e) by using the 'miracle question' (see Figure 6.2). Each of these in-session behavioral management interventions will be briefly described in the next section.

Triangling self into the couple's argument and creating physical distance between partners   refer to decreasing the conflict by having the couple talk to the counselor rather than to each other, and to placing more distance between the partners during the session.

Keeping score or having payment made for critical comments   refers to using some method of recording points whenever one partner offers a put-down or criticism of the other, or to each partner paying the other whenever she or he feels criticized.

Using a paradoxical intervention   when the counselor questions whether a couple want to give up a timeworn aspect of their relationship.

Remembering exceptions to escalating conflict   refers to having clients identify behaviors they have used to avoid nonproductive conflict.

Using the 'miracle question'   refers to having the couple halt their symmetrical pattern, asking them to consider how they would like their relationship to be, and having them consider what they as individuals could do to bring about this relationship.

Figure 6.2   *Interventions for destabilizing a symmetrical relationship*

Triangling Self into Arguments and Creating Physical Distance. By triangling herself or himself into a symmetrical argument, the counselor can reduce the intensity of the conflict as the couple talk directly to her or him rather than to each other. Each partner still hears their mate's remarks but gives the counselor her or his thoughts rather than sending them to the partner and escalating the conflict. In the example of Tom and Sharon, each could be offered an opportunity to talk with the counselor.

Counselor: Tom, tell me more about what visiting your in-laws is like for you.

Tom: Well, whenever we're at Sharon's parents we simply stay at their house and sit in the living room and hear about relatives or talk about the neighbors.

Counselor: I can hear that has been anything but enjoyable for you. How would you like to spend time when visiting Sharon's parents?

Tom: There are plenty of things we could do. We could go into the city and see a show or simply visit one of the museums.

Counselor: Have you talked to Sharon about this?

Tom: Seems like whenever we try to discuss it we get caught up in an argument.

Counselor: Sharon, I thought I heard you saying you felt the need to spend time with your folks and felt cheated because Tom wasn't interested.

Sharon: I do feel cheated. We spend time at Tom's parents but he can't seem to give up time to be with my family.

Counselor: Evidently the relationship with your parents is important to you and you'd like Tom to appreciate it.

Sharon: That's right. The older they get I realize we won't have that much more time together.

By the counselor being empathic and helping each partner explore their position on an issue, the old symmetrical pattern of interacting can be brought to a stop and the intensity of the conflict can be lowered. Once the intensity of the conflict is lowered, the couple can again be instructed to reach an agreement on visiting extended family members.

In a similar manner, Minuchin and Fishman (1981) have commented on how physical distance can be related to emotional distance, and this observation may be utilized as the counselor has the conflict-laden couple sit further apart from each other.

Counselor: Sharon and Tom, let me ask you to move your chairs so that they're about six feet apart.

This physical distancing may bring about the emotional distancing needed to de-escalate the conflict and interrupt the symmetrical pattern.

Keeping Score or Having Payment Made for Critical Comments. By keeping score we mean that the counselor may want to place a chalk mark on a blackboard below each partner's name whenever one of them offers a put-down or criticism of the other. This type of score keeping sends a message that competitive attack and counterattack scenarios really do not produce a winning relationship. An alternative to score keeping, and an intervention that is even more behavioral in nature, is to have each partner bring a roll of coins to the session and to pay each other a coin each time one of them feels criticized by the other. Piercy (1983) described this 'penny game' as a variation of a procedure outlined by Watzlawick, Weakland, and Fisch (1974) for destabilizing attack and counterattack patterns of interaction. In order for this to work, the one who has felt criticized merely has to hand a penny to their partner. Let's use Sharon and Tom's case as an illustration:

> *Counselor*: I'm going to give each of you a roll of fifty pennies. I'd like you to continue discussing how visits with your parents can be worked out and during this discussion, whenever one of you feels put down by the other, I want you to give your partner a penny. I'd like you not to make a comment when you give the penny. Simply hand one over to the other person. Let's do this for the rest of today's session, and whoever has the fewest number of pennies at the end of today's appointment wins.

This behavioral intervention relies on the couple's competitiveness. We do not attempt to alter the couple's competitive style through this intervention. Rather, we try to capitalize on it by making their competitiveness work for rather than against their relationship. It is when they stop the verbal attacking behavior that they stop receiving pennies and, as a result, win the game. This intervention may destabilize old patterns of interaction, thereby setting up the possibility that the couple will be more receptive to alternative styles of interacting.

The Paradoxical Intervention. The paradoxical intervention helps the couple encounter the futility of the attack and counterattacking or debating relationship. Papp (1981) suggested at least three components of a therapeutic paradox: (a) the couple's problem (attacking behavior) needs to be defined as an essential part of the relationship, (b) the attacking pattern can be prescribed as an essential part of the relationship and, when the couple show signs of change (decreased conflict), (c) they need to be cautioned to slow down their movement toward change. Weeks and L'Abate (1982) commented on paradoxical prescriptions and descriptions and noted that a paradoxical description also has three components: (a) the couple are told how the counselor likes their pattern of behavior e.g., 'I've been impressed with your willingness to hang in there for one another,' (b) the polarization (or we would suggest any sequence) in the relationship is described e.g., 'Each of you has been committed enough that you've tried endlessly to correct and improve the other,' and (c) the counselor asks the couple if they are happy with this relationship e.g., 'Why should we try to change your relationship?'

The following illustration considers components of prescriptive and descriptive paradoxical interventions, as well as Andolfi's (1980) notion about prescribing dysfunctional rules.

> *Counselor*: You know, you've previously mentioned a desire to decrease your debating and arguing. I, however, might question the wisdom of this decision. I would wonder if the debating and arguing doesn't really allow for a much sought-after closeness for each of you. Why try to change something that's been so important to you?

If the couple recoil and object to the counselor's comments, the counselor may respond by encouraging the couple to go slow in thinking about change. We have found this intervention to be helpful with couples who express a desire to change and, yet, also indicate that the symmetrical escalation of conflict seems to be beyond their control. If they indicate that there must be another way to remain close in their relationship, the counselor has an opening to introduce an alternative style of interacting.

Remembering Occasions that were Exceptions to Escalating Conflict. Minuchin and Fishman (1981) as well as de Shazer (1988) have talked about helping clients use unrecognized strengths for resolving presenting problems. Minuchin and Fishman suggested that individuals may withhold competent ways of functioning for relationships outside the family and suggested procedures for helping clients demonstrate more functional patterns of interacting, while de Shazer has asked clients to pay attention to what they are doing when presenting problems are not present in their lives. We, in turn, have also asked couples to focus on those times when they have sidestepped an escalating power struggle.

> *Counselor*: Let me stop you for a moment. It looks like we could get into one of those disagreements that escalates out of control. In the past, what have you found helps in sidestepping arguments where nothing gets settled and where bad feelings get generated?
>
> *Sharon and Tom*: [*Quiet and no response*]
>
> *Counselor*: Alright. Would you be willing to do an experiment?
>
> *Sharon*: Okay.
>
> *Tom*: Sure.
>
> *Counselor*: I'd like you to slowly take three deep breaths and on the third breath, as you slowly exhale, close your eyes. Now, search through the past week and remember a time when you successfully avoided getting caught in an unproductive argument. When you've recalled a procedure for avoiding this type of conflict, open your eyes.
>
> *Tom*: I remembered last Saturday, we were in the kitchen, and almost ended up in an argument over our summer vacation plans. Do you know what I'm talking about?
>
> *Sharon*: I sure do.
>
> *Tom*: Well, when I saw it wasn't going anywhere I went upstairs to work with our computer. Nothing was settled but at least there wasn't a blow up.
>
> *Counselor*: So when you felt things weren't going to get resolved you got busy with something else. How about you, Sharon?
>
> *Sharon*: I remembered Sunday night when we started to disagree on plans for the weekend. I suppose, like Tom I could see the discussion wasn't going anywhere so I got busy with something else. I think it was sewing.
>
> *Counselor*: Excellent. So you both have the ability to read a situation and ask yourself if an issue is really worth arguing over.
>
> *Tom*: I guess so.
>
> *Sharon*: The problem is that we don't do this often enough.
>
> *Counselor*: Okay. Let me ask you to do something else. Again, take three deep breaths and as you exhale from the third one close your eyes. Now think about some one at work or a friend you've been with when you found yourself in disagreement and yet worked it through without a series of explosions. What did you do that helped you handle that

situation? When you've thought this through open your eyes.

Sharon: I remembered last week. Mother wanted me to spend some time with her but our son had his first baseball game and I simply told her how important it was for me to see him play. When I explained my feelings about being there for him she understood.

Counselor: So explaining your feelings instead of becoming confrontive with her was important. How about you, Tom?

Tom: Well, my boss had an idea for the office that I didn't think would work and I could tell that his idea would mean some inconvenience for me. It looked like he had made up his mind so I decided to go along with his plan and see how it turned out. It was tempting to tell him what I thought of his idea.

Counselor: So you could see that this idea was important to your boss and instead of getting confrontive you decided to save the relationship by letting him play out his idea. It looks like you've both found ways to sidestep escalating conflict. You've mentioned asking yourself whether the issue is worth the conflict and, if not, getting busy with something else or saving the relationship by playing out the other person's idea and, if the issue is important, explaining your ideas and feelings rather than becoming confrontive. Now, I'd like you to take these skills you have and again discuss how you're going to handle spending time with your parents.

In fact, it may be that a couple have skills for negotiating escalating conflict but reserve them for extrafamilial relationships or have simply lost sight of them. Stopping the couple as they begin to spiral into conflict, and helping them focus on skills they have used for negotiating conflict may assist in destabilizing a symmetrical pattern. We will now turn to a final destabilizing procedure from the large number of possible in-session behavioral management interventions.

The Miracle Question. The miracle question (de Shazer, 1988) with a magic wand adaptation (O'Hanlon & Weiner-Davis, 1989) can be used as a behavioral management intervention for bringing escalating symmetry to a momentary stop, and the following might illustrate our adaptation of these interventions.

Counselor: I'd like you to stop for a moment. You've both mentioned that your arguing and debating style have been counterproductive for the relationship and, yet, you've found it all too easy to continue criticizing and trying to push each other into changing. I'd like each of you to turn your chairs toward me. Let's suppose that I could give each of you a magic wand and let's suppose that with a wave of this wand you could change and improve your relationship. The question I'd like each of you to answer is, 'What would you, not your partner, find yourself doing differently as you interact with one another to bring about this new relationship?'

Again, this behavioral management intervention focuses on bringing a momentary end to escalating conflict. It also attempts to refocus the couple's attention away from 'What my partner needs to be doing' and towards 'What I could be doing to improve the relationship.' Often, within the question, the statement is found that suggests that the present condition of the relationship is, in part, determined by how each partner behaves.

Of course, there are an infinite number of in-session behavioral management interventions and counselors should be encouraged to come up with interventions that fit the particular cases with which they work. Also, many of the interventions just described as appropriate for symmetrical relationships could also be adapted to complementary relationships and vice versa. It needs to be remembered, however, that the purpose of these procedures is to challenge the redundant patterns of behavior that have interfered with the couple resolving disagreements and organizing their relationship in a more equitable fashion. Furthermore, it may be helpful to remember that the thoughtful delivery of an intervention may heighten its effectiveness. We will next discuss the delivery of a behavioral management intervention to block or destabilize redundant and problematic patterns of interaction, and we will present more lengthy illustrations of procedures used to interrupt complementary and symmetrical patterns.

Preparing the ground
When using some behavioral management procedures, the counselors may want to preface the intervention with a few questions and instructions. First, see if the couple will agree that a particular pattern of interaction (such as complementary or symmetrical pattern) is a problem and, second, find out if the couple would like to stop engaging in their destructive pattern of interaction. Finally, the counselor may want to see if the couple will agree to carrying out the in-session behavioral management intervention before it is delivered, or have the couple explore the

'negative' consequences of changing their pattern of interaction prior to instructing them in a behavioral management intervention. These techniques are used to heighten the couple's commitment to following through with some behavioral management intervention.

The technique of securing an agreement from the couple before the intervention is described has been referred to as the 'devil's pact' (Watzlawick, Weakland, & Fisch, 1974). Counselors may find the 'devil's pact' helpful prior to using a stop watch to control time or prior to providing payment for critical comments and there are a number of considerations in this 'blind commitment' step. The counselor may want to mention that a commitment to carrying out an intervention needs to be seriously considered. Sometimes a solemn delivery is helpful in increasing the seriousness with which the couple make that commitment.

If the couple agree quickly to the commitment, it is helpful to slow the process down and to ask each of them if they are really committed to carrying out this 'blind commitment' and to changing their relationship. If the couple do not agree to making a 'blind commitment,' the counselor might say something like, 'That is probably wise. You may not be ready to change quite yet.' This statement is designed to reinforce the wisdom of the couple and to sidestep resistance that may occur in relation to the counselor. If the couple agree to the 'blind commitment,' we have found they are likely to complete the task. The counselor might indicate that she or he has confidence that the task can be helpful but also indicate that whether it is helpful or not is really up to the couple. Again, we want to express hopefulness to the clients, but we do not want to take responsibility for the success of the intervention. To 'guarantee' success seems only to encourage the clients to show the counselor that her or his ideas were not appropriate. When agreement to the 'blind commitment' is not reached, we have found that couples will often agree at a later date because they are curious about the nature of the therapeutic task.

Finally, once agreement to a 'blind commitment' is established, the counselor can proceed to providing the couple with a directive designed to destabilize their accustomed pattern of interaction. Illustrations of the 'devil's pact' will be provided in this chapter.

We have also found it helpful to use a procedure described by Weeks and L'Abate (1982), to increase motivation for complying with a destabilizing intervention. In using this procedure we discuss the 'negative' consequences of change with the couple prior to instructing them in a behavioral management intervention. Counselors may find this technique helpful prior to having partners consider 'What would it be like to be married to me?', prior to asking them to remember exceptions to escalating conflict, or prior to using the 'miracle question.' Here, the couple are told that change can have both positive and negative effects and that the counselor wants to be certain that the price of change is worth it to the couple. So, the counselor discusses with the couple the 'negative' consequences of change. However, these consequences are actually the beneficial results of change but framed in a negative manner. As an example, Weeks and L'Abate provided a description of the 'negative' consequences of change for a man with a long history of depression: he would be able to make friends but it was noted that this could be stressful, he would want to be more assertive and responsible in his marriage but it was noted this would deprive his wife of things to do, and he would be able to be closer to his children but it was noted this might lead to saying no to some of their requests and conflict. The following is an illustration of discussing the 'negative' consequences of change prior to introducing a behavioral management intervention.

> *Counselor*: You know, whenever you change a pattern where one person has been active in problem solving and the other has been more removed and passive, there is always the possibility of experiencing negative as well as positive consequences. Can you think of any negative consequences of changing this active–passive pattern of decision making?
>
> *Roberta and Franky*: [*Quiet and no response*]
>
> *Counselor*: Well, what if changing your relationship required Franky to get more involved in decision making? Could this be a negative consequence?
>
> *Franky*: It would be what's needed. Often Roberta is left making all the decisions and I'm left not knowing what's going on.
>
> *Counselor*: So maybe that's not a negative consequence of change. What if change requires Roberta to give up some responsibility for decision making so that Franky can become involved? What do you think about that?
>
> *Roberta*: That might be.
>
> *Franky*: The positive thing is it would lead to more communication instead of just watching TV when I get home.
>
> *Roberta*: Well I'm not sure. I have a difficult time keeping my thoughts to myself when Franky's talking because he often says something that gives me an idea and I want to say it right then and there.
>
> *Counselor*: Perhaps what we're saying is that giving Franky

time to participate in decision making would be a negative consequence of change.

Roberta: No, I don't think so because I want him to be able to say what's on his mind.

Counselor: Then, perhaps, giving Franky time to participate won't be a negative consequence of change. What if you got closer together through sharing in decision making? Perhaps that's a negative consequence of changing this pattern. You see, I want to make sure that the price of changing this pattern isn't too great for you.

Roberta: No, I've always wanted to be closer and to feel the closeness of us talking together. It makes me feel more affectionate.

Franky: Yea, more closeness would be fine.

Counselor: Okay, it sounds like the two of you have decided on working towards change. [*Counselor then delivers a behavioral management intervention designed to destabilize the relationship pattern during the session.*]

Illustrations of destabilizing

Complementary Case. When couples present in ways where one partner appears dominant and the other acquiescent the counselor's task is to interview in a manner that challenges the relationship. The following case represents such a challenge.

Rose and Norman Bustle presented themselves for couples counseling after 12 years of marriage. Rose had become pregnant shortly after the couple graduated from high school and Patsy was their oldest child with nine-year-old Willy being the youngest. Since the beginning of their marriage Rose had worked as a teacher's aid while Norman had found a clerical job in the local library with additional odd jobs during evenings and weekends to help support the family. The couple noted Norman's occasional loss of temper as their presenting concern. They also clarified that Norman's anger was restricted to verbal criticisms of Rose or Patsy. He described himself as a worrier and noted that he worried about a variety of issues including bills, Patsy becoming a teenager, and relationships with extended family members. Over the course of the first few sessions it was discovered that Norman also procrastinated with responsibilities at home and, in recent years, Rose had become more involved in paying bills, parenting, and scheduling the family's social life. Norman also mentioned that the further removed he became from the family's decision making, the more worrying he experienced and, with the worrying, eventually came a verbal explosion. Moreover, the couple seemed to interpret Norman's explosions as a sign of his inability to handle responsibilities at home.

When the counselor asked Rose and Norman to discuss and resolve a concern in their relationship (paying bills), a pattern developed where Rose talked to and informed Norman about how procrastinating with bills placed the family in financial jeopardy. Of course, Norman agreed with Rose's analysis but found it difficult to change his behavior. During these enactments a complementary pattern was demonstrated where Rose outlined the importance of resolving various problems that were pressing on the couple and Norman passively listened. As a result, the presenting problem (Norman's verbal explosions) was viewed as a mechanism for maintaining the couple's homeostatic pattern of behavior. That is, Norman's explosions were interpreted as evidence of his inability to handle responsibilities at home and, as a result, it did not seem unusual to observe Rose lecturing him on the importance of problem solving and to observe Norman remaining disengaged. In this complementary pattern of interaction, Rose would be described as the competent partner and Norman as the non-involved mate. What follows is a description of how the counselor could use the stop watch intervention to destabilize this complementary pattern.

Counselor: We've been talking about keeping episodes of anger under control and I've been wondering how that's been going.

Rose: Things have been pretty good lately.

Counselor: Fine. The pattern I thought you'd been describing was one where Rose had been active and helpful with solving problems at home and Norman had been more disengaged and passive. It seemed that during this disengagement and passivity Norman would worry about family problems until an explosion would occur. These explosions could occur around parenting issues, paying bills, decisions about spending time with extended family members, or just about anything.

Rose: That's right.

Counselor: What we've been trying to do is develop another pattern where Norman would become more involved in decision making and Rose would give up some of this responsibility. Is that what you've seen us doing?

Norman: Yup. That's right.

Counselor: Okay. Let's take another look at that. Is there a decision coming up in the near future where the two of you need to reach an agreement?

Rose: Yea. There are a couple of them.

Norman: What are you thinking about?

Rose: Well, one issue has to do with a program for teenagers that our community is developing.

Norman: Right. The community needs people to help with this project and Rose would like us to become involved.

Rose: We've been kind of pushed into this.

Norman: With my second job, Patsy starting piano lessons, and Willy's schedule, I'm thinking there isn't enough time for this.

Counselor: Okay. I'd like you to consider doing an experiment that may help in changing the pattern where Norman becomes disengaged and passive and Rose assumes responsibility for the decision making. But before I can tell you what the experiment is, I need your promise to participate. It's something that could be helpful but whether it is or not is really up to you. If you're willing we will do the activity in our session today, but I need a commitment from both of you that you will participate in the experiment before I can tell you what it is.

Norman: I'd be willing.

Counselor: You know, changing how you relate to one another can be somewhat unsettling and so a commitment to the experiment is important.

Rose: Yea. It would be okay.

Counselor: You're agreeing pretty fast to do this.

Rose: Well, I'm not saying it will be easy or that I'm not scared but I'll try.

Counselor: Well, I've come to know you both in the past few weeks and I have the impression that you're people of your word. That is, I think when you give your word it means something. So you think we should go ahead with this experiment?

Rose and Norman: Sure.

Counselor: I brought this stop watch along and I'm going to set it in front of you. I'd like one of you to pick it up and give yourself 60 seconds in which to tell the other person whether the two of you should get involved in this community activity. When your 60 seconds is up, give the watch to your partner and she or he then has 60 seconds to respond to your comments or to share her or his thoughts about whether you should get involved. Even if you run out of things to say before your time is up, hold on to the watch for the 60 seconds. I'd like you to continue passing the watch back and forth until you come to an agreement on whether you're going to get involved. So, whoever wants to start, pick up the watch. [*During the following discussion between Norman and Rose, the couple keep exchanging the stop watch.*]

Norman: I just feel that we better not commit ourselves to something we can't do well. We already have enough on our hands and I worry that we would burn ourselves out.

Rose: Well, I think I would like to get involved and I'm not saying you have to. I just want to be there to help out. I know pretty soon, when Patsy gets old enough to be part of this program, I can't be in the group and, so, now is the time for me to do it.

Norman: Well, I would propose, with our busy schedule, that you get involved with the program and I'll get involved in special time with Patsy and Willy at home. I just think both of us getting involved right now, with all the other things we're doing, would be too much. It would put me in a panic if we were both involved in the program.

Rose: Well, I agree. I think your idea would be really good. I spend much of my time at home or at work and sometimes I need time away. So I feel that you being home with Patsy and Willy would be great.

Counselor: When either of you thinks you've reached an agreement say to the other person 'I feel like we've settled this. Do you agree?'

Rose: I think we reached a settlement. Do you agree?

Norman: Sounds good to me.

Counselor: What did the two of you think about that exercise?

Norman: I liked having time to talk. Also, sometimes we don't always listen to the other person before we begin talking and the stop watch gave us time to talk and listen.

Counselor: What did you think, Rose?

Rose: I liked it. I really did.

Counselor: I thought you did a tremendous job and I'll tell you why. First, when some couples try to settle an issue they get sidetracked on to other concerns and never resolve the presenting problem but this didn't happen to you. Next, I thought it showed a lot of maturity for Norman to say 'I don't want to be involved in this activity but I'm okay with you doing it.' Sometimes it's alright for partners to do different things. It also showed real maturity for Rose to say 'Yea, I'm okay with that too' and it doesn't have to mean that you're angry with each other or that you don't care for each other. Now, you also said that there was another issue that needed to be discussed.

Rose: Well, Norman's parents have invited us to go to the farm with them but Patsy and I really don't like staying there.

Norman: See, my folks invited us to go with them as part of a birthday party but my daughter doesn't like it. She complains about the lake water being cold and the farm being in the country away from her friends.

Rose: Plus, I'm not sure that I could go because I've promised to help one of our neighbors. We don't do much together but when she asked me to help her this weekend I said okay.

Norman: I feel that we should go to the farm as a family but Rose has resisted this.

Counselor: Okay. Let's try the procedure with the stop watch again. I'll place it between you and whoever would like to start can go first. [*Again, the couple keep exchanging the stop watch as they discuss their concern.*]

Norman: I just feel that we should all go to the farm as a family and have a good family time. I simply don't want to hurt my parents' feelings. They're doing something nice for us and I don't like making excuses. Maybe I should tell them the truth that Patsy just doesn't want to go but making excuses makes me feel uncomfortable. I think it would be a good time and I think she really could enjoy it.

Rose: Well, I can understand Patsy's feelings. I feel the same way she does, and right now I don't want to be with your parents. They've previously said how disappointed they are in us and besides I just don't care for going to the farm. [*Here, there is a suggestion that Norman's parents are triangled into Norman and Rose's marriage.*] Besides, if we're going to go at 5:00 and be back by 11:00 for church the next morning it's going to be too late for me.

Norman: I think there are times when you and Patsy need to put aside your feelings about not liking the farm and think about how Willy and I enjoy it. [*Norman's comment suggests a possible coalition between him and Willy and another one between Rose and Patsy.*] Having family time together can be pretty neat. Plus it's a good opportunity to work on staying out of conflicts when Mom and Dad say something that irritates us. Personally, I really like the farm and think the four of us could have a fine time. I just want to have some family fun together.

Rose: Well, I understand your need for us to do things as a family but sometimes each of us needs to understand that the other person would rather be doing something different. We don't always need to be doing things together as a family. Patsy and I were talking last week about doing something together, but then it got canceled and the weekend after this one has already been scheduled. So this Saturday Patsy and I would like to go to the movie rather than to the farm.

Norman: I think you and Patsy could go to a movie during the week and then we could have this Saturday as a family time. You need to think of what others want to do. Patsy perked up when she heard about the birthday party. I know she would have a good time.

Rose: Well, during the week our days are so busy that the only time she and I have together is Friday night and that's reserved for basketball games, and sometimes we do go to the games as a family. It's not that we don't enjoy being together as a family, it's just that I don't want to be with your parents right now.

Norman: Well, if you and Patsy are bent on not going I suppose we've hit on an impasse. Maybe you could call Mom and Dad and tell them who will be going to the farm. I think that's one of the biggest problems, calling Mom and Dad and telling them only some of us are coming. It's like, 'What do I say?' But to break this impasse I guess I'll go along with you two going to the movie Saturday night.

Rose: Well, you've got to realize there are a lot of things your parents don't show up for. As the kids are getting older and their interests change, the four of us won't be doing as much with your folks. Patsy has said she feels too old and mature for birthday parties.

Norman: I can think, however, of one problem. If Willy and I are going to the farm, you'll need to go to the early show so that we can leave on time.

Rose: That's fine and you can explain to your parents that Patsy and I had made other plans ahead of time, before their invitation. Patsy has been bugging me to see this movie with her and I had promised we would do it this weekend. It's not that I just don't want to be with your parents but often when we're with them they get critical of us and I'm stuck having to defend our family.

Norman: I never thought of that. I'm okay with you and Patsy going to the movie. I think we need more of these sessions so we can sit down and discuss these issues.

Counselor: How was that for the two of you?

Rose: Well, harder than the first time.

Norman: I don't know. After going back and forth for so long I felt frustrated.

Counselor: I know when couples have strong opinions compromise sometimes doesn't seem possible and the best outcome is accepting that my partner has a position different from mine. But the thing that impressed me was that as you began to see that you weren't agreeing you continued to present your thoughts instead of quickly giving in to please the other person. Another important moment was when Norman told Rose that he was struggling with letting his parents know that the family wouldn't be going to the farm. Rose needs to know how you feel in order to help you with planning family activities. I thought she gave you some ideas about how to explain the decision to your parents.

Norman: Yea, she did.

During the stop watch activity in the above session it appeared that Norman was more verbal than usual in helping Rose with decision making. It may be that the stop watch became a vehicle for Norman's new level of involvement. Use of the stop watch appears to give each partner a chance to express opinions on issues like how to spend time (say, with friends or relatives) and sends a covert message that each needs to be involved in decision making. Being given the stop watch and 60 seconds challenges the old rule in Rose and Norman's relationship that only one is to behave in a responsible manner and make decisions for the family while the other is to behave in a more incompetent manner and not be involved in decision making.

Minuchin and Fishman (1981) suggested that some couples simply need a gentle nudge to change while others tenaciously cling to old patterns of behavior. The structure provided by each of the abovementioned behavioral management interventions is intended to bring these old patterns to a halt. Moreover, the behavioral management interventions may also help the couple experience the controlling power of their old and accustomed patterns of inter-action. For instance, had Norman not been so active in decision making and had he sat in silence while holding the stop watch, it is our belief that both he and Rose may have experienced and felt confronted with the nonproductiveness of their accustomed pattern of interaction.

Symmetrical Case. The second set of behaviors that sometimes must be managed is that of couples who are locked into patterns of symmetrical, escalating, mutually abusive verbal attacks. The task of the counselor is to break into the attack and counterattack cycle so that the redundant pattern becomes destabilized. In the following case, Piercy's (1983) 'penny game' is used as a means of managing 'put-down' behavior in sessions.

The Fireflys, Blaze and Brandie, had been married seven years. Blaze was a high school principal 44 years old with grown children from a previous marriage. He worked long hours and had a 100 mile round-trip commute to work each day. This was Brandie's first marriage. She was 32 years old and worked at a local hospital. Brandie first called for counseling and reported that she was depressed, that she did not enjoy work, and that she was having some concern about her marriage. Both wife and husband were asked to come to the first session.

Brandie was timely in her arrival for the session but Blaze who was driving directly from work was about 20 minutes late. Brandie was upset about Blaze's late arrival and started the session by accusing Blaze of not caring about her or the marriage as evidenced by his lateness. Blaze countered by saying that she did not care about him or she would consider that he didn't have a job that could be stopped at a specific time. He then proceeded to tell how he had been working with a distraught child and that he could not just have left at 3:30 p.m. Brandie indicated that he had known about the child for days and that he could have worked with the child two days ago. The session continued in this vein far longer than was necessary for the counselor to diagnose the repeated pattern.

Although the content of the second session shifted, the attack–counterattack pattern continued. A variety of techniques were used in an attempt to alter the pattern: explaining the pattern to the couple, giving them a directive to 'make something different happen,' and urging them to argue more. None of these approaches was able to stem the battle for long. Finally, about 15 minutes into the second session the counselor decided to use the 'penny' technique in an effort to stop the attacking pattern so that the couple might move to a different level of discussion. The following is an abbreviated description of how the 'penny' technique could be introduced to Brandie and Blaze in order to help destabilize their symmetrical pattern of interaction.

Counselor: Brandie and Blaze, we have talked before about your pattern of constantly attacking each other. That seems to be a problem to me, does it seem that way to you? Does it make your sharing of concern for each other difficult?

Brandie: It sure does.

Blaze: Yup.

Counselor: I think it's a problem and that it's disturbing enough that it would be helpful if you would stop beating on each other. Do you want to do something about it?

Brandie: We sure do.

Blaze: You bet. That's why we're here.

Counselor: You've been committed to your ways of fighting for a long time. It's almost like each of you has ears with a full-time channel tuned to criticisms. Yet, you are here, you seem to want a relationship that works, and you seem to really care about each other. I have something for you to do that I think will stop your constant criticism of each other and allow your caring to come through. It's something I'd like you to do for the rest of today's session. Of course, whether the activity works or not is really up to you, but I'm pretty sure it will help. You, however, have to agree to do the assignment before I will tell you what it is.

Brandie: We agree.

Counselor: You may want to think about this a little more. It's a pretty serious thing to think about changing your relationship; that is, to think about not attacking and counter-attacking.

Blaze: We'll do it.

Counselor: Okay. I'd like you to discuss how more caring and demonstrations of interest and concern for each other can be injected into your relationship. Also, I'm going to give each of you a roll of fifty pennies. When you feel that you are being put down by your spouse, I want you to give your partner a penny. I'd like you not to make a comment when you give the penny. Simply hand one over to the other person. Okay? Let's do this for the rest of today's session, and whoever has the fewest number of pennies at the end of today's appointment wins.

Brandie: Well, I think increasing our time together might be one way of showing interest in each other.

Blaze: I also enjoy our time together. It just seems that with all the demands at school it's been difficult to plan activities.

Brandie: You just need to decide which is more important, Blaze, your family or your job.

Counselor: How do you feel about Brandie's comment, Blaze?

Blaze: Attacked and criticized.

Counselor: Okay, then, give Brandie a penny.

Brandie: I was just telling the truth.

Counselor: What we're interested in is who will be able to get rid of their pennies first. Why don't you continue.

Blaze: I think we should consider how to increase our time together. Perhaps we could do a better job of planning enjoyable things to do when time allows. We both like to go for walks over at the arboretum.

Brandie: I'd certainly like to do that some time. What about this Saturday?

Blaze: You know we're getting ready for our accreditation visit at school and Saturdays this month have been set aside for that work. You're continually putting me in difficult situations and then become critical when I don't respond as you'd like.

Brandie: Here's your penny, Blaze. [*Brandie looks at the counselor with a smile.*]

Counselor: Seems like you've got the idea, but simply hand the other person a penny without commenting on the process.

Blaze: Looks like we're going to need to think about what we say to one another.

Brandie: Yea, but I still would like to figure out a way so that we could be together this weekend.

Blaze: [*Quiet and no response*]

Brandie: I won't complain if you wanted to stay longer at work Friday evening. Then maybe you'd be able to be home from school by noon on Saturday and we could go to the arboretum.

Blaze: I think I could do that.

As indicated in the above illustration with Blaze and Brandie, if the symmetrical behavior continues in the session and the partners are not extending pennies to each other it is best to assume that they did not realize they were attacked. For the counselor to simply say, for example, 'Did Blaze just put you down?' will often activate the realization process. A little coaching will also often provide the impetus that allows the in-session behavioral management intervention to be effective. We have found that couples will often end the session with about an equal number of pennies.

Summary

Counselors need a repertoire of in-session behavioral management interventions for challenging impasses that develop during the counseling session and, again, these impasses may be manifested as complementary or symmetrical patterns of interaction. It is because these patterns have become rigid and redundant sequences of interaction that couples experience difficulty in resolving issues in their relationship, and it is because couples tenaciously hold to these patterns that they become impasses in couple's counseling. We view techniques such as the stop watch intervention and the 'penny game' as resources for counselors to use in managing the couple's behavior during the counseling session. Counselors will obviously want to come up with in-session behavioral management interventions that fit the particular cases with which they work. Let us now turn our attention to out-of-session interventions that are designed to support work started during the counseling session.

7

Managing Out-of-Session Behaviour

The time that couples spend between counseling sessions can be used for evaluating their interactions and for trying out or solidifying new and more helpful behaviors. Unfortunately this out-of-session time also provides opportunities for the repetition of old dysfunctional behaviors. The repetition of these dysfunctional patterns results in frustration, discouragement, and despair. Worse, occasionally repetition of the negative patterns results in violence, abuse, threats, endangerment and other behaviors that diminish the couple's esteem and vitality. The counselor's role is to help or collaborate with the couple to increase their adaptive, functional out-of-session behaviors and to help them decrease and in some cases eliminate dysfunctional behavior patterns. A major tool that counselors and couples use to manage out-of-session behavior is homework. Homework consists of those activities and behaviors a counselor encourages, suggests, requests, or requires a couple to engage in between counseling sessions.

Often both the task of homework and the process by which the task is to be completed are prescribed by the counselor or planned by the couple and counselor. This homework is designed for the purposes of helping a couple to better understand their relationship, to offer encouragement by providing success-oriented experiences, to introduce new behavior into their relationship, and to solidify functional behavior patterns. This chapter is about ways of using homework to help couples manage their out-of-session behaviors. Homework can be considered along two dimensions. Counselors provide homework to couples that offers them the opportunity either to *think* about their situation in new ways or to *behave* in different ways. Obviously, most homework has both 'think' and 'do' components. The homework may also have either *overt* or *covert* aspects or both overt and covert aspects. We are using the term overt to refer to homework in which the intent of

The 'Metaphors and Rituals' section of this chapter was constructed from an article written by the authors et al. that appeared in *Individual Psychology: The Journal of Adlerian Theory, Research & Practice*, 47 (2), 1991 (see References).

the intervention is known to the couple, such as communication training, while covert interventions refer to those in which the intent of the homework instructions is not made known to the couple, such as metaphors. It should also be noted that homework may be given to the couple as a unit or to either partner as an individual.

We are also often asked about how to make decisions regarding specific homework assignments. This question seems to focus on making sure that the homework addresses the essential problem that the couple are experiencing. Luckily, our own experience indicates that such specificity is not required to provide helpful homework to couples. First of all, many solutions to couples' problems do not directly involve the presenting complaint; rather, the solutions come from assisting couples in applying common curative factors to their relationship: noticing positive behaviors, listening, taking action, etc. Secondly, homework should generally be aimed at reducing imbalances and polarizations that couples experience. It is not as though there is a central core problem that has to be addressed, rather there are usually extreme ways of thinking (making meaning) and acting that need to be reduced and altered so a couple are not so limited in their ways of relating. We would believe that homework is designed to change behavior and/or thoughts (meaning), that it contains both covert and overt components, and that it introduces curative factors and reduces polarizations and imbalances. Haley (1987) used terms similar to overt and covert homework when he noted that directives for action can be either direct (straightforward) or indirect. We will now consider overt and covert homework interventions that are designed to be influential in the couple's relationship between the counseling sessions.

Overt Homework

This homework may include training, guidance, ordeals, as well as absolution-gaining directives (see Figure 7.1). All of these activities involve a shared understanding between the counselor and the couple as to the goals of the homework.

Training Couples in Relationship Skills
There is a sense in which all that counselors do is training. By attending to specific verbal and nonverbal behavior they are training or educating couples about what the counselor thinks are important aspects of their relationship that need to be heightened or lessened. When a hand is raised as a gesture for a spouse to be

1	Training couples in relationship skills
2	Providing guidance or advice to couples
3	Therapeutic ordeals
4	Paying penance and granting absolution

Figure 7.1   *Overt homework*

quiet, the counselor is training both spouses to notice boundaries and perhaps to listen. Either through a verbal prompt or a gesture motioning the client to speak, the counselor trains couples to address that which was previously barely noticed. This training of clients to attend to the stimuli around and between them may be the essence of counseling. It is one of the methods counselors use to stimulate new behavioral sequences. Education is sometimes defined as 'shining a light upon' or 'illuminating' and in this manner counselors are truly educators. They train a light upon aspects of a couple's relationship that are already present and that offer them hope and solution.

At times counselors impart information directly to couples. In this activity they are also educators or trainers. They may teach spouses how to be assertive, how to listen for meaning, or how to use the steps in a problem-solving sequence. Often these activities will be practiced in the counseling session. They may even be used to manage behavior in a session but ultimately, if couples are to reap maximum benefit, the skills must be employed in the couple's life outside the counselor's office.

When a counselor trains by illuminating aspects of a couple's relationship, it is not necessary for the couple to know the goals of the illumination. However, when a counselor trains spouses in skills such as problem solving, listening, etc., it is important that the couple not only have an awareness of the goals of the training but that they also agree that the training will be helpful. Thus, the training takes on an overt behavioral quality. Usually, such training takes place in-session and proceeds to follow-up homework designed to reinforce the in-session experience. For example, a counselor might teach listening skills to a couple by having one speak and the other indicate what they have heard via paraphrasing. For a homework assignment, the counselor might ask the couple to sit back-to-back and ask one of them to share for ten minutes their thoughts and feelings relative to the relationship or dreams for the relationship. The counselor would then instruct the listening spouse to report, in no more than five minutes, what they had heard. The speaker would be given a two-minute opportunity to clarify any points misunderstood by the listening spouse. After that, the speaking and listening process would be reversed and repeated. Often this speaking and listening assignment becomes a success experience, a beacon of hope, for spouses who have had difficulty communicating with each other. The counselor can assist the couple in having a successful experience by defining success as completing the exercise with each having said something mean-ingful and each believing that the other heard what was said.

Likewise, assertiveness can be practiced via homework and yet under the control of the counselor. Again it is helpful to practice the assertiveness activity in the laboratory of the counseling session before it is practiced at home. Helping the couple see that both settings are experimental in nature will increase their ability to learn from the activity.

Joanne and Fred had been married for 12 years and they reported that sex had been a source of stress between them for most of those years. They indicated they had sex only about once every other month, sometimes less, but there was a felt tension between them almost every day about whether or not they would have sex that night. Fred said that despite their past he still spent energy trying to establish conditions so that Joanne would want to have sex, and Joanne mentioned that she also would like to have sex more often but felt that her desire to have sex was on trial each day and so found it difficult to say yes to Fred. It was as though she was always reacting to Fred rather than having any wishes of her own. Although making the decision to have sex had been stressful for a long time, Fred and Joanne had not discussed the problem.

The counselor responded to Fred and Joanne's expressed desire to increase the frequency of their sexual activity. He also assisted them in realizing that they never asked if the other was interested in having sex, and they were helped to realize that neither had ever said 'yes', they would like to have sex or 'no', they would not like to have sex. He gave them the following prescription over a three-week period. The prescription was given one week at a time and thus the couple were not aware of what would be prescribed in succeeding weeks. They were told, however, that the prescriptions would take place over a three-week period and they agreed to this treatment approach.

For the first week, Fred and Joanne were told that they were not to have sex. They were told that they could be affectionate with each other but, of course, this was not required. Fred and Joanne returned for the follow-up session and reported a pleasant week. Joanne indicated she had felt better all week. She had enjoyed her work and the children and she even indicated some fun times with Fred. Fred was not as excited as Joanne but he too said that the week had gone well. Interestingly, much of the session had a positive tone and little time was spent discussing their sexual concerns. The counselor learned that he could probably use a more direct approach in working with the couple because they had reportedly followed his earlier directive. (At other times couples have responded to the 'no sex' directive by having sex and usually the counselor has had to move to a more covert treatment approach.)

For the second week, in consideration of the couple's stated desire to increase their sexual activity and in an effort to stimulate more forthright communication between the couple, they were given the following directive. During the week Fred and Joanne were to have sex two times. Joanne was to initiate sex, that is, tell Fred that she would like to make love, and Fred was to decline at least two times. Fred was not to initiate lovemaking or indicate to Joanne in any other way than through a response to her initiative that he desired to have sex. An explicit direction was given because the couple had demonstrated a tendency toward compliance by following instructions the previous week. This particular prescription was used because it reversed the couple's usual roles (Fred initiating and Joanne declining), because it eliminated anxiety about how often they were to make love, and because it required the spouses to be more direct in their communications about lovemaking.

At the next session Joanne and Fred again indicated that they had completed the assignment. They were satisfied with the results and somewhat surprised by what they had learned. Joanne indicated that she was relieved that she didn't have to feel angry or guilty because she didn't respond to Fred. She said she felt like she had been on a vacation. Fred said that having sex twice during the week was plenty, maybe even too often, and that he was glad he had been given 'veto power.' Joanne was surprised and relieved at his disclosure. She said that part of her fear had always been that if they started to make love more often that there would be no end to Fred's desire.

Because the couple reported the second week's activity as being helpful and because direct, assertive communication was still a goal, the second week's prescription was repeated but reversed, with Fred initiating and Joanne both refusing and accepting. Although the couple had indicated making love twice a week might be too often, they were again told to have sex two times to see if it really was too frequent.

Fred and Joanne reported that the week went well. Their tone conveyed that sex was really not a big issue for them. The counselor checked on the couple's satisfaction with the sexual aspect of their relationship in future sessions but the couple never reported problems. The counseling continued with the focus shifting to getting to know each other again. In relationships where one or both partners lacks assertiveness skills, there is an opportunity to initiate a 'falling-in-love again' atmosphere. This is so because as the partners become more assertive they disclose more personal information. This self-disclosure is often met with enthusiasm and interest.

The prescription of practicing direct communication methods is used frequently to help couples manage out-of-session behavior. We have seen many variations in the responses of couples. The counselor needs to anticipate these responses so that all can be viewed as helpful. The key to viewing homework as helpful is to relate whatever happened to the clients' acknowledged goals, then the results can always be viewed as a learning experience. If the couple were better able to manage their relationship via the communication practice, they would probably report a success. However, if the homework was not completed or did not result in better management of their marriage, the couple could still be asked what they learned about themselves and their relationship through the assignment. For example, a couple with a complementary style were given an assignment that better balanced their household responsibilities. When they returned the couple reported that only one of them had completed their portion of the assignment. However, they both mentioned a greater awareness of their overfunctioning–underfunctioning relationship and thus the learning was viewed as meaningful.

Providing Guidance or Advice to Couples

Frequently, couples are in need of guidance or advice about issues in their lives. This guidance might pertain to seeking further information from appropriate sources or it might take the form of providing advice about a particular set of circumstances.

Some couples need professional services in addition to counseling. These services might be of a legal, medical, financial, safety or specialized treatment nature. Counselors need to be alert to symptoms of clients that might warrant a referral. In addition to advising clients of the need for assistance from other professionals and service providers, it can often benefit clients to give advice relative to the conduct of their daily lives. Guidance regarding daily living may easily fall within the expertise of the counselor. For example, if a couple report that they experience a great deal of unwanted interference from one or both sets of their parents, it is sometimes helpful for the counselor to advise them to develop a stronger boundary (gain more distance) from their parents. Such advice may seem needless because it may appear obvious to the counselor that such distancing is the solution to the presenting problem. Yet such a solution may not be obvious to the clients, since they may have been more concerned with expressing their misery than involved with finding a solution to their problem.

There are three important factors to consider when providing advice: guidance is provided most effectively when it is sought; advice that furthers the couple's goals is more readily accepted than advice that counters their goals; and advice concerning what to do, when to do it and how to do it are separate but related processes. While unsolicited advice is usually not welcomed by anyone, there are exceptions to this maxim. For example, a client might welcome advice to see a physician when a counselor is aware of symptoms that might suggest the presence of a medical condition. But in general, counselors are better off giving advice only when it is requested or when they can entice the client into seeking their opinion. This latter condition might be achieved by making a statement such as: 'I have some ideas about what you might do. Do you want to know what they are?' If the couple seem hesitant about responding the counselor might say, 'It seems as though you might be hesitant about what I would share and that's certainly okay.' Conveying respect for the desires of the couple is an important aspect of gaining their confidence. Again, it is usually wiser to refrain from sharing unrequested advice.

When giving guidance to couples, the advice will be most readily accepted if it can be related to the goals of the couple. For example to say, 'I've been very impressed by your concern for your children and your desire to be good parents. I think that given the goals you have, it would not be helpful to your children for them to be home alone all week while the two of you are vacationing' is probably more acceptable than saying, 'I think either one of you needs to stay home or you need to get another adult to stay with them.' In the first instance the advice is clearly related to the couple's goals. In the latter, the advice seems more parental and often such advice will meet with resistance. Usually, the counselor only needs to confirm advice that the couple give to themselves. In fact, often a couple only want confirmation of something they have already decided to do. The key for the counselor is to ascertain in which direction the couple is leaning. The 'couple's leaning' can usually be found by asking, 'What do you want to do?' or 'What do you think you should do?' Then the counselor can simply say, 'Given what the two of you say you want to have happen, it sounds like you've given yourselves good advice.' If the couple's advice to themselves does not in fact seem helpful, that too, can be mentioned, 'Given what you say you want to have happen in your relationship, I'm not sure that the course of action is going to be helpful to you. You might want to consider. . .' Again, relating the advice to the goals of the spouses is important.

When advice is given that results in a decision by a couple to pursue a course of action, that decision is only a small step in the change process. Counselors err when they believe that a couple's choice to pursue a course of action represents a culmination of counseling. They fail to realize that helping the couple to decide how and when they will act, taking the action and, then, evaluating the outcome are all important aspects of the counseling process. For example, a couple may decide they are going to establish a firmer boundary between themselves and their parents, but that decision will not usually result in the formation of a new boundary. There are still issues about who should be present when parents are talked with, who should talk, what to say, and how to respond to the parent's hurt and angry feelings. A role play of the confrontation may be helpful and the role play may need to contain scenes of what could go wrong in the discussion with the parents. Spontaneous confrontations seldom represent a new behavior for the couple and seldom result in lasting change.

In summary then, when providing guidance to couples about actions they could and maybe even should take in their lives outside the session, it is important for counselors to remember that choosing actions, timing actions, and taking actions are all separate steps in a process. Each step must be given consideration in both the planning and conducting of the counseling session, and all must again be given consideration in evaluating therapeutic outcome.

Therapeutic Ordeals
A third type of overt intervention with couples is what Haley (1984) terms therapeutic ordeals. Ordeals may be provided to

couples in either an overt or covert manner. In either case the prescribed behavior would be presented in detail to the client but, if one were prescribing a covert ordeal, the client would not necessarily be informed of the hoped-for behavior change. Covert ordeals will be discussed as part of paradoxical interventions later in this chapter. Congruent with Haley's definition, an ordeal is a prescription of a behavior that will be more aversive, more distressful to the client than the behavior it is designed to extinguish. One makes continuance of the symptomatic behavior contingent upon performance of the ordeal behavior and, if the ordeal behavior is more aversive than the symptom, the symptomatic behavior will cease.

Gary and Sandra came to counseling after about two years of marriage. Gary was in his mid-thirties and highly successful as the head of a small stock brokerage firm. Sandra was in her early twenties and was attempting to finish her college education. Gary was highly critical of Sandra and voiced disapproval of her childish friends, her lack of knowledge about how to run a household, and her penchant for soap operas. His criticism included a great deal of name-calling involving disparaging sexual terms. Sandra became quite upset by Gary's language and insinuations and Gary was not able to stop his behavior. It appeared that Gary wanted to be the head of the household and when Sandra challenged his leadership, to the extent that he became anxious, he would reassert himself by verbally belittling her. Both Gary and Sandra agreed that the name-calling was not helpful and Gary agreed to try to stop this behavior.

The following ordeal was prescribed. Gary worked in an upmarket downtown office building. He perceived that his image with his supervisees and the community was very important to the success of his brokerage firm. Two doors down from the entrance to the office building was a storefront radical left wing bookshop, a place in which Gary said he would not want to be seen. The counselor's directive was that if Gary were to refer to his wife in her presence, using any of a pre-established set of words, he was to leave work fifteen minutes early the next day and spend 45 minutes, at the close of the business day, standing in the front window of the bookstore reading an easily recognized 'left wing' newspaper. Thus he was to be in the window from 4:45 p.m. to 5:30 p.m. while many clerical workers and his business associates passed by. Further, if any coworkers mentioned seeing him in the window, he was to indicate that he thought that the literature in the store was valuable. The counselor emphasized that Sandra was to decide if any of the 'banned' language had been used and that Gary had to carry out the 'ordeal' if she so indicated.

The result was that Gary in fact spent 45 minutes in the store the week after the prescription had been delivered, but he had not faced the street. The prescription was repeated for the second week with the provision that he had to be facing out the window. As it turned out, he did not have to repeat the ordeal behavior for the length of the treatment.

As indicated earlier, Haley (1984) stated that the magnitude of stress caused by the prescribed behavior must be greater than either the distress or the benefit caused by the symptom. He also stressed three other points: (a) that the ordeal must be something the person can do, (b) that the acceptance of the ordeal or at least the idea of performing an ordeal is voluntary, and (c) that the ordeal not be harmful to the client or others.

Haley recommended several steps that must be taken in prescribing an ordeal. Because the ordeal is to follow a problematic behavior, the problematic behavior must be defined carefully so that the client knows when the problem is occurring. Next, before an ordeal can be successfully prescribed the client must be committed to getting over the problem. For a counselor to attempt to solve a problem that is either not acknowledged or determined by the client to be worthy of solving, is to pursue a usually futile course. An ordeal must be selected and it is important for the client to collaborate in the generation and selection of an ordeal sufficient to overcome the symptom. At the same time that a 'sufficient' task is selected, attention can also be given to assuring that the ordeal would benefit the person. The ordeal must be precisely prescribed and attention needs to be given to what is to be done, when it is to be done, and for what duration. A rationale for the activity needs to be given, and this can usually involve the idea that doing something that is harder on oneself than the distress caused by the symptom will eliminate the symptom. The ordeal needs to be continued until the symptom is eliminated and, if the symptom does not disappear quickly, the length of time the ordeal is performed can be extended or the frequency of performing the ordeal can be increased.

Finally, Haley (1984) indicated that the impact of the ordeal will often extend beyond the symptom area. For example, in the above case the ordeal was a part of redefining the relationship between

Gary and Sandra on a more egalitarian basis. The task sensitized both Gary and Sandra to the superior–inferior balance that was present in their relationship. Sandra seemed to be empowered by being taken seriously and Gary became sensitive to the basic dignity of another human being. Thus, not only was a specific problem of language use eliminated but the balance in the relationship was addressed as well.

Often both spouses play a part in maintaining the couple's presenting problem and, thus, ordeals can be simultaneously prescribed to both partners. Giving each spouse a prescription helps define the problem as being dyadic or systemic in nature rather than residing in the lap of only one individual. Again, in prescribing couple ordeals, the task is to find a behavior that can be prescribed to the couple or each spouse that is more aversive than the behavior to be eliminated.

Paying Penance and Granting Absolution

At times counselors can be helpful by playing part of the role of a priest: one who hears confession, prescribes penance, and declares forgiveness. At least counselors can facilitate the confession–penance–moving-on-with-life process. While forgiveness is not always necessary in a couple's relationship, the ability to 'move on' is essential.

Homework aimed at absolution is most appropriate in situations where one partner is perceived to have wronged another and the couple or a spouse is unable to move beyond the 'wrongdoing.' Expressed difficulty in moving beyond the 'wrongdoing' is the key in determining when an absolution-gaining directive might be given. At times the issue may lie with the wrongdoer who is unable to accept or forgive the wrongdoing. Sometimes, in such instances, the 'victim' is not even aware of being a victim. On the other hand, the issue may also be of concern to the victim who wishes for punishment or revenge against the 'perpetrator.' When a partner has been wronged it is helpful to ask what their mate must do to pay for the victimization so that life can go on. And, once the penance is carried out, the couple may seem more open to exploring other pertinent issues in their relationship. In the following case a ritual was used, as suggested by Haley (1984), to allow the couple to move beyond accusations about their past.

Cathy and David came to counseling with the asserted goal of finding out if they should get married. They had lived together for about four years and, although there had been considerable turmoil during these years and they still had doubts, they thought perhaps it was time to get married. Both had come from problematic families. Cathy seldom saw her family and was resentful that her parents showed very little interest in her child from a previous marriage. David had a history of substance abuse with the drugs being supplied by his mother and brother. Needless to say, he had frequent contact with his family. Cathy was resentful and distrustful of David and of his family.

The couple consistently, both in-session and out-of-session, made accusations concerning the other's past. They had met at a time when Cathy had recently been sexually assaulted by an acquaintance. David at that time showed concern for Cathy and her child, and about three months after the relationship began, David moved in with Cathy. The relationship was defined as Cathy being needy and David being a 'savior.' However, in exchange for the 'tremendous service' he was providing to Cathy, David decided he deserved to have an affair. He thus began a relationship with a former girlfriend. When Cathy discovered this relationship she felt angry and hurt. She felt deceived in her relationship with David. As a way of rebalancing the relationship, Cathy, with David's covert approval, decided to have her own affair. This relationship, however, was upsetting to Cathy and did not even the score with David. Although all this had occurred about three years previously, the couple still made frequent accusations to each other about these past events.

The prescription given the couple in the fifth session focused on eliminating accusations concerning their past relationships. The couple agreed that the accusations were not helpful and indicated their desire to discontinue their verbal attacks. Each was instructed to write, on separate sheets of paper, five accusations that they were willing to give up. They were to bring these written accusations to the next session along with a sealable glass jar.

The following week David and Cathy arrived at the session with five accusations each and the glass jar. However, instead of writing five accusations they were willing to give up, they had written accusations they wanted their spouse to give up. Although the counselors had been explicit in providing instructions, the counselors indicated the error had been theirs and that they had not been clear in providing the homework. Throughout the session the couple fell back into their accusatory behavior. The counselors used this accusatory behavior to help the couple solidify the view that the accusations were not helpful, and the original prescription was given again at the end of the session.

David and Cathy came to the seventh session with the accusations 'correctly' written and they also brought back the jar. David and Cathy were instructed to alternately read the accusation they were willing to give up and to place them in the jar. Each time they repeated the following, 'I _____ will not in the future accuse _____ of . . .' They were then instructed to get a shovel and the following Saturday go to a favorite spot and bury, at least four feet deep, the jar containing the accusations. They were to rid their life of these behaviors. However, they needed to keep a record of where they had buried the jar because if at any time in the future they returned to their accusatory behavior they would need to recover the jar as a symbol of their broken promise.

Cathy and David indicated in the eighth session that they had gone for a picnic on Saturday and buried the jar in a place that was very special to them. They had purchased a new shovel for the occasion, painted it gold and hung it above their bed as a reminder of their promise. Accusations were not a problem in future sessions and David and Cathy also reported a more cooperative environment at home.

About six months later David became re-involved in drug use and the old accusatory behavior returned. Cathy and David were instructed to get up at 6 a.m. the following Sunday morning, a time they liked to sleep, and recover the jar. They did so. David again dealt with his substance abuse problem and the couple decided to marry about three months later. The accusatory behavior did not resurface and the couple indicated they took monthly picnics at the site of the burial of their past accusations as a way of celebrating their new life. One could describe this case from a metaphorical–ritualistic perspective. However, it was important to the couple to both exact and pay a price for their previous wrongdoings. By giving up their accusations, Dave and Cathy paid for the opportunity to establish a new relationship.

The management techniques discussed as overt procedures to be used with couples all have covert aspects. It would seem, however, that the intent of these homework assignments has been made known to the couple. Often couples do not respond to overt directives in ways that increase their well-being. Their response may reflect the tension they have with each other or with the counselor. In such instances, more covert assignments may be indicated.

1	Paradox
2	Metaphors and rituals
3	'Alien' directives
4	Doing nothing

Figure 7.2 *Covert homework*

Covert Homework

Covert homework involves the denial of some aspect of a therapeutic message. Andolfi et al. (1983) noted that any therapeutic message is composed of four parts: (a) the counselor, (b) says something, (c) to a couple, (d) in a therapeutic setting. When an indirect homework assignment is given, the counselor denies one or more of these components: (a) that she or he sent a message, (b) that a particular message was being sent, (c) that the client was the desired receiver of the message, or (d) that the message was aimed at therapeutic change. For example, when a metaphor is used, there may be a denial that a therapeutic message was sent, that there was any intent to the 'story', and/or that the couple were the intended recipients. The vagueness which surrounds indirect directives may allow couples to receive therapeutic messages that they may have resisted when the intent of the message was made known. Covert homework assignments may include: paradox, metaphors, 'alien' assignments, and doing nothing (see Figure 7.2). These assignments may at times include providing clear and direct instructions about what is to be done with little if any indication of why it is being assigned.

Paradox
Much has been written about the use of paradoxical interventions in couples and family counseling. Detailed descriptions of the types and subtleties of these covert interventions have been provided by various authors (Selvini Palazzoli et al., 1978; Papp, 1981; Weeks & L'Abate, 1982). These works may be referred to for refined explanations of the nature and use of paradoxical interventions. In Chapter 6 we discussed the use of a paradox in the management of in-session behavior; here we will discuss paradox as a way of managing out-of-session behavior. In essence, a paradoxical intervention involves the counselor questioning whether a couple

should let go of a behavior pattern that they have acknowledged as counterproductive to their relationship.

Counselors often switch to using covert interventions after more direct interventions have failed. The failure of direct interventions, those where the goal and the method of achieving the goal are clearly described, may lie in the couple's resistance to direction from the counselor. In addition, failure to complete the task or to accept the intended benefits of the task may come from the polarization that exists within the couple's relationship. For example, couples will engage in a kind of challenging behavior whereby each says, 'I'm not going to change until you change.' Consequently, they remain deadlocked with no one being able to move. Or, at times, couples engage in escalating arguments. Both members often acknowledge that the arguments are not helpful and yet direct efforts to get them to stop do not result in de-escalation. In such instances, we, and others, have found that paradoxical prescription of the symptomatic behavior may bring relief. If the couple are in a resistive mode, then instructing them to perform the problem behavior (continue complaining about one another) may escalate their resistance beyond a point with which even they are comfortable (Andolfi, 1980). The following case scenario illustrates the use of a paradox for managing out-of-session behavior.

Linda and Scott had been married for about 7 years and had daughters four and two years old. The reported symptomatic behavior in their relationship was arguing. Their style was to fight symmetrically. In session they demonstrated this behavior repeatedly. If Linda would say something was black, Scott would talk about how it was really more white. If one thought that some degree of success had been gained in disciplining the children, the other would raise points to show that either the gains had not been made or that their partner was filled with false hope. At intake, Scott and Linda indicated they would like to decrease their fighting behavior. In their goal setting (see Chapter 3) they saw fighting as their primary problem and indicated that they argued in about 75% of their communication. The counselor proceeded to use some basic relationship training techniques during treatment. Linda and Scott would practice communication skills in-session but they did so only with a great deal of monitoring and coaching by the counselor. They did not report any improvement in their out-of-session behavior. By the fourth session the counselor realized that the direct intervention technique was not going to work and decided to use a paradoxical approach.

Initially, following Papp's (1981) suggestion, the counselor defined the problem in a benevolent manner and as an important part of the couple's relationship. He then proceeded by prescribing the paradoxical intervention.

Counselor: You know, we haven't gotten very far in working on your problem of fighting. I don't know why, perhaps because I like you both so much, but it has taken me a while to understand the importance of your fighting to you. I'm sorry I've been a bit slow. I know that your marriage means a lot to you and now I can see that fighting is really your way of communicating intimately with each other, of letting each other know how important the other is to you. I've been working to take something away that is very dear. I see how important it is to you and yet it wears you out. I want you to look a bit closer at this fighting so that it can become even more meaningful. I have something I want you to do this week that might help you, of course it might not, but I want you to do it. You say you fight about 75% of the time, that would be about five days a week and that seems to be about enough for you. You may need to increase it, but at least for right now, I think that is enough. In order to take a closer look at this, I want you to fight on five days but only five days. You need a break on a couple of days to kind of re-arm yourselves. Now you can decide which five days. You may want to fight five straight and then give yourselves a break or you may want to fight two days take one off, fight two more and take one off and then come back for a final round. You don't even have to both fight on the same day. Anyway, you figure that out. Do you understand the instructions? Okay, see you next week.

The following week, Linda and Scott came back and reported they had fought a couple of days but that the counselor's instructions had not been followed. They had a comparatively quiet week and had gone out and bought a couple of board games. Linda and Scott had enjoyed board games early in their marriage, but had forgotten how much fun they were to play. The counselor appeared somewhat disappointed and indicated concern that they were losing something, their arguing, that was important to them. He said he didn't think that was a very good idea. In succeeding weeks Scott and Linda continued to reduce their nonproductive arguing. The counselor continued to be pessimistic. In a final session the counselor admitted that Linda and Scott had stopped their arguing and asked what they had done to bring about this change. He said he needed to learn from them so he might use their ideas with other couples.

Several aspects of the case illustrate important ideas relative to the successful use of paradoxical interventions. As in all interventions, it is important to frame and label behavior, whenever possible, as having a benevolent quality. In this instance fighting was labeled as a way of gaining intimacy. Secondly, it is important for the counselor to have conviction, to believe in what she or he is doing. The pacing, tone, and delivery of the directive is very important. In this instance the counselor requested the couple to engage in the fighting behavior rather than suggesting the behavior or requiring the behavior. Suggestion was considered to be too mild and requiring the behavior would not have allowed paradoxical change to occur. Finally, when the paradoxical result was reported it was important for the counselor to remain dismayed and doubtful about the continuance of the new behavior. If the counselor hints that she or he knew this improvement would happen the stage is set for the couple to resist by getting worse. If the counselor is congratulatory and begins a treatment process to further the gains, the couple will often regress to their problem behavior.

Frequently, counselors have difficulty with the ethical dimensions of paradoxical and other covert interventions. If they consider their task to be the stimulation of change and to seek the well-being of their clients, and if they estimate the likelihood of success in using only direct insight-oriented approaches to be low, then they often feel a sense of commitment to learning indirect interventions.

Metaphors and Rituals

A second category of covert interventions includes the use of metaphors and rituals. Metaphors and rituals, as indicated in Chapter 5, can assist couples in developing more helpful conceptualizations of their relationship. They can also be used to provide signposts to couples on how to relate outside the counseling session.

Metaphors are used in couples counseling to denote a likeness between the couple or one of the spouses and another object, person, figure, or action. This likeness between the client or situation and the metaphorical symbol provokes a perceptual change which can facilitate problem resolution. Prescriptive metaphors, then, are indirect interventions whereby stories are developed by the counselor consistent with the couple's dilemmas. The stories are delivered to the couple and offer solutions to problems or guidance for the future. Relatedly, therapeutic rituals have been described as being held together by an underlying guiding metaphor (Imber-Black, Roberts, & Whiting, 1988), and the metaphor is symbolic of some relevant couples issue. The metaphor acts as a guide for indirectly experiencing the themes, issues, and dilemmas facing the couple (Anderson & Stewart, 1983; Gordon, 1978). Some couples, for instance, regularly allow a spouse to overfunction, whereas other couples vie competitively for control. Indirectly experiencing themes such as overfunctioning or competition, via the activity of a ritual, facilitates an alteration in the couple's perceptual predisposition so that they may begin to live new solutions to old problems (Lankton & Lankton, 1983). The following case as well as the comments on metaphors and rituals draw directly from an earlier article (Bubenzer et al., 1991).

Mary and Bob, both 23, had been married about 15 months when Bob called the clinic to inquire about couples counseling. Over the phone Bob indicated he did not want to make the appointment, but his employer suggested he give us a call. Bob mentioned that on his first wedding anniversary he realized he no longer wanted to be married. Bob still wanted to be able to 'run around with the boys, drink, and play pool.' The couple were invited for an initial 'exploratory' session. A male and female counseling team was used.

Because of the length of the marriage, initial hypotheses about tasks to be addressed in counseling included: (a) the need for separation and appropriate distancing from families of origin, and (b) the need for joining and accommodating to one another. In other words, it was thought that the couple could more adequately differentiate themselves from their families of origin and establish a more appropriate level of marital intimacy.

The initial session confirmed these hypotheses. Bob was in fact living at home with his parents who looked after him, and reportedly attempted to create an environment in which he could 'think through whether or not he wanted to be married.' Bob voiced displeasure with his parents' protectiveness but used their services. Much of his after-work time was spent 'drinking and riding motorcycles with the boys.' Mary was living in the couple's apartment but indicated she was considering moving out, so Bob might return and have more time to think about the marriage. In the initial sessions, Bob dominated the conversation, speaking approximately 80% of the time about his unhappiness in the marriage, his desire to be free and to do things his way, his problems with his parents, and his guilt feelings about how he was leading his life. Mary often wept quietly, talked very hesitantly about her anger, indicated she had great concern for Bob, and mentioned she knew how difficult this was for him.

Treatment strategies revolved around the issue of separation from parents and accommodation to each other. To a lesser extent Bob's relationship with friends was addressed. We thought the couple would benefit if Bob would become less self-focused and more interested in knowing Mary. In a complementary fashion we thought it important for Mary to make herself knowable, to make a statement about herself to which Bob would respond. The treatment strategy involved four major ritualistic or metaphorical movements.

The first therapeutic ritual was delivered in the third session. Mary began by complaining about Bob's father who was always giving marital advice and she began by berating Bob for never standing up to his father. We thought Mary was figuratively saying, 'Bob, I need to be more important than your parents, please declare yourself for me.' Toward the end of the session the treatment team said they wanted to think for a moment and left the session. The team returned about ten minutes later with this assignment: Bob was to state to his parents, with Mary present, that he and Mary wanted to handle their marriage together and they wanted his parents to stop advising them. We thought this encounter needed to be a planned, nonspontaneous act, so that there would not be a 'telling-off' exchange. Since clients often resist this type of high-anxiety assignment, we asked them to promise to carry out the assignment before we indicated what they were to do (devil's pact). The following week Bob reported feeling uncomfortable in completing the assignment, but he had, and his parents had, in fact, stopped advising. Mary was pleased with Bob's action.

The first therapeutic metaphor used in treatment contained what Barker (1985) termed a relationship metaphor; that is, one relationship (the counselors') becomes a metaphor for another (the clients'). By the sixth session the treatment team had noticed a repetition of in-session patterns where the male counselor talked with Bob for most of the time. The therapeutic team's interaction was a mirror of the client couple. A goal of counseling was to address the accommodation between spouses by helping the male client to get to know his wife and by helping the wife to make herself more knowable. Yet direct efforts to encourage the wife to talk more had failed. Mary feared that if she shared herself, Bob would be alienated and probably leave the marriage.

When the pattern of Bob and male counselor dominating talk time repeated itself in the session, the counselors said they were stuck and needed some help. They asked Bob and Mary to reverse roles (therapeutic reversal) with them, with the counselors playing the clients' roles in a manner that demonstrated the couple's relationship. The male counselor (husband) explained his difficulty in making a decision concerning the parents' overprotectiveness, and the female counselor (wife) talked timidly about her hesitancy in making demands and requests in the marriage because she wanted the best chance of the marriage continuing. Thus, the role play was a mirrored metaphor for the clients' relationship. During this role play the wife began to cry and the counselors returned to the therapeutic role with the female counselor taking the lead by saying, 'Mary, we spend a lot of time attending to and taking care of Bob, so do you, and so do his parents. Who takes care of you?' The wife tearfully began to talk about herself and her need for involvement with her husband. The husband accommodated by listening and later sharing that he thought Mary was right about what she had said.

At the close of the sixth session we prescribed a ritual with a metaphorical meaning that once again addressed separation and accommodation issues. Mary was graduating from a business college in the forthcoming week, and her mother and relatives were coming to the ceremony. We asked Bob to plan a celebration for Mary that would take place in the presence of the entire family, but only he and Mary would know the celebration was occurring. We also indicated he should plan a celebration that would be pleasing to Mary, and not necessarily pleasing to him, but planned in such a manner as to celebrate for and with Mary in ways she would understand. We thought it important to allow Bob his 'I'll do it my way' approach but to channel that style in a manner that attended to Mary's needs. At the following session he reported buying a gift for Mary's graduation, but more importantly, he had worn his wedding ring to graduation as the 'secret' celebration. After family celebrations were over, Bob and Mary went out together. In addition, he moved back into the apartment with Mary.

For the eighth session we designed two alternative plans. One plan was to be used if Bob and Mary had distanced since the previous sessions, and the second plan would be used to encourage intimacy if they were still moving in a 'together direction.' They came to the session and stated that they were doing quite well. As a result, we designed the following metaphorical story to deal with the complexity of the accommodation and separation themes. Brief relaxation techniques, breathing exercises, were used before telling the following story.

> This is a familiar story; we've all heard it and even lived it. It's about a boy whose Mom and Dad decided they were going to take him on a vacation. He really didn't want to go, but you know how it is when you're a kid, you sometimes have to do what Mom and Dad want. He didn't want to go on vacation because he had to give up his baseball season. He was a popular player but was afraid if he left now he'd lose his spot and the team wouldn't want him any more. Mom and Dad won, however, and they all went on vacation. On vacation, he found a beach to walk. At first he didn't like the beach that much, but it allowed him to get away from Mom and Dad. He was resentful and sometimes he'd tear up the sand by dragging his foot. Sometimes he'd drop cans and trash on the sand. And yet, the beach was forgiving. The tide would come up and wash the marks away and the cans would be gone, and he began to get interested in knowing the beach. As he began to know the beach he began to care for it. He discovered the beach had a personality; sometimes angry and stormy, sometimes calm and gentle. As he began to care for the beach, its beauty came forth. He saw it as a place to play and a place to think, a place to share his fears and joys and, in turn, the beach shared back.
>
> As time went on he cared for and protected the beach. He even brought his parents to see the beach. They saw his joy in the beach and decided they needed to enjoy their own vacation because he was okay. He began to know and discover the beach even more, and they were together in ways they had never known before.

The couple were then instructed to go home and write letters to each other indicating the behaviors of their spouse that they appreciated, behaviors they desired, and what each felt she or he wanted to give to the marriage. They were instructed to live out their letters but to not discuss them. In the following session both partners indicated that the relationship was going quite well. Mary indicated how much she appreciated Bob taking time with her and listening to her. They also indicated that Bob's parents had been less intrusive and even cited an example of Bob's father starting to give advice but then stopping himself.

Certainly, there were aspects of Bob and Mary's case that were nonmetaphorical. We, however, felt that the metaphorical and ritualistic interventions had a very positive impact on helping the couple alter their at-home behavior. The prescription to Bob to plan a celebration for Mary's graduation that was shared secretly by them, but took place in the presence of the larger family context, appeared to impact the couple's separation and accommodation issues. Bob chose to wear his wedding ring as a part of the 'secret' celebration. Within the week of the celebration, he moved out of his parents' home and moved in with Mary. After the delivery of the 'beach' metaphor, Mary became more assertive in the counseling sessions. She spoke more freely of her goals and of her frustrations with Bob's behavior. In response to Mary's sharing, Bob became quieter and expressed interest in Mary's views. The couple were seen three times after the 'beach' metaphor was delivered and reported high marital satisfaction. A three-month follow-up was also positive.

As noted briefly in Chapter 5, our metaphor or ritual creation process begins with identifying dynamics in the couple's relationship such as repeated cycles of unproductive behavior, typical ways of approaching problems – symmetrical, complementary, etc. – and ascertaining each spouse's affect. Thought processes can often be hypothesized from the affect of spouses. For example, if a member reports feeling lonely, we may hypothesize that she or he desires a more companionable or appreciative spouse. We then construct a metaphor or ritual with images that utilize the repeated behavior cycles, that recognize and challenge the thought processes, and that offer alternative solutions to those the couple has considered.

Barker (1985) suggested that the planned metaphor will not seem so strange to couples if stories, anecdotes and illustrations are used throughout the counseling process. We tend to use metaphors at the beginning or at the end of sessions. At the beginning they set a tone for the session, and at the end they stimulate a preparedness for the coming week that helps the couple manage their relationship between appointments. Clients seem to respond better to a longer metaphorical story if they are relaxed when it is delivered. The delivery, the pauses, and intonation the counselor uses in sharing the metaphor are all important. It is helpful for the counselor to have practiced the delivery of the metaphor prior to the session. When a metaphor is delivered at the end of a session, as a parting message, we usually terminate the interview soon after delivery. We do not spend a lot of time processing the metaphor because to do so seems to lessen the benefits of the metaphor, as indicated by Andolfi et al. (1983). That is, processing the metaphor eliminates the counselor's denial that she or he has sent a therapeutic message to the client. Often, counselors want to follow up on the impact of the metaphor or ritual. In doing so, we think it is important that the couple do not perceive that the counselor is trying to teach them something. When they suspect teaching, they will sometimes become resistant. We might have introduced the metaphor by saying, 'I'd like to share a story with you that came to my mind this week' and in the follow-up we might ask, 'What does this story say to you?' If the couple do make a connection between the metaphor or ritual and their own situation, the counselor may demonstrate interest, attribute the connection to couple insight, and emphasize the importance of the connections.

Metaphors do have an impact. It is not unusual for couples to use the language of the metaphor in future sessions or to begin attending to aspects of their relationship in ways prescribed in the metaphor. Frequently, couples will even ask if they can have a copy of the story and they are flattered that the counselor took the time to create a special story just for them.

'Alien' Directives

'Alien' homework, that which is foreign to the thought or behavioral processes of the couple, can be helpful in increasing problem-solving behavior. This seemingly absurd homework tends to work best with couples who exhibit highly polarized behavior or where at least one of the spouses lacks spontaneity and is very thoughtful, precise, and measured about their life. With the polarized couples the homework involves asking them, 'as just an experiment,' to think or behave in ways different from their highly polarized positions. For the 'irresponsible' member, the prescription might be to develop a carefully planned schedule, where they can contemplate the appropriateness of specific behaviors, where they can reflect on their attire or consider how their money is spent, etc. Although the assignments may appear to be quite overt in nature, they usually do not seem so obvious to clients. Again, the counselor does not make the purpose of the activity clear to the couple. Those clients who approach life in a scientific and logical fashion often benefit from adding flexibility, humor, and an element of casualness into their lives. Such an expansion, to include the spontaneous and informal aspects of life where complete control is not needed, allows couples to relinquish some of their intense feelings of responsibility, to see spouses as equal and responsible persons, and to increase the boundaries of what is acceptable and even enjoyable about their relationship. Alien directives may seem absurd to the couple and can be given to either one or both parties in the relationship.

Often an introductory phrase, such as, 'You may think that what I'm going to tell you to do is strange, but I want you to do it anyway' is helpful in stimulating clients to complete the directive (Haley, 1976). Or, one might say, 'You know the usual in life but I'd like you to tackle the unusual.' Such a directive is most often given after the counselor has gained the trust of the client, and with precise, hesitant clients this may take a few sessions. For these controlled clients the directive should be provided in a very measured, minutely exact manner, matching the thinking, emotional and behavioral style of the client. The reason for providing the directive or the intended objective should not be divulged. If inquiry is made, it can usually be deflected with a response such as, 'You know it sounds strange to me too and I'm not sure what the result will be, but I want you to do it anyway.' Invariably, such clients find a purpose in doing the activity and come back changed. In what we would consider a typical covert strategic directive a client might be asked to drive a very precise distance from home, say 2.4 miles, stop the car and sit for a specific length of time, say 12 minutes, and discover a reason for doing the activity. Varying the routine of someone who has a very precise and regimented schedule may prove helpful. Such a person or couple might be asked to change their time of awakening, mealtime, or bedtime by a specified period and report what happened.

George and Charlotte had been married for 10 years. George was a salesperson who always feared that the bottom would fall out of his sales territory in the succeeding month. Accordingly, he planned his week very carefully, allowed clients to take advantage of him, and used spare time, a concept foreign to him, to catch up on paperwork. At home, on weekends, he always involved himself in a set of preplanned tasks that kept him occupied from sun-up until bedtime. He also was disparaging of Charlotte for not being so driven. Charlotte was upset not only by George's lack of involvement in their relationship but also by his badgering of her to be equally task-oriented. George's unrealistic fear of the failure of his sales efforts had been discussed and he was urged to reward himself by taking a vacation from his frenetic behavior but no change occurred. Finally, an alien task was prescribed. The counselor brought a medium-size stone to the session and gave it to George with the instructions that George was to arise at least 20 minutes earlier than usual on four mornings during the following week. He was then to sit in his favorite chair for 16 of the 20 minutes and hold the stone in his hand. He was told that this was to be a solitary activity and that he should do the activity four mornings for 16 minutes, not any more or any less. The morning was prescribed because George had indicated he was a 'morning person.' The counselor indicated he wanted George to do the homework when he was at his brightest. George was told that he would need to report what he had learned the following week.

George returned to the next session and said not much happened the first day but by the second day he began to notice the intricacies of the stone. He then proceeded to describe the color, shape, and texture of the stone with great detail. When asked what he thought of all this, George indicated that he thought there was much more to his life that he ought to get to know. In succeeding weeks he began to be more attentive to Charlotte, to listen more carefully to what she had to say, and to get to know her in ways that his pace and sense of responsibility had previously prevented. A seren-dipitous event occurred in this case that seemed to have as great an impact on George as did the alien homework. About a month after termination George suffered a severely broken ankle. He was confined to home for one week and limited in his travels for over a month. Later George called to say that his time at home had provided him the permission he needed to slow down.

Certainly, not all alien directives result in such positive and dramatic changes as those for George and Charlotte. Yet almost always, the activities are related to change that can be framed in a helpful manner.

Alien directives take on metaphorical qualities for the client but they differ from other metaphors created by counselors. The effort is to create an event disconsonant with the usual; that is, a crack in a very structured way of interacting and yet a crack that provides the client with a great deal of control. Thus the activity does not have metaphorical intent for the counselor. Absurd direc-tives can be very enjoyable to prescribe. They must, however, be prescribed with sincerity and honesty and for the well-being of the client. Nothing should be prescribed that is illegal or that is potentially harmful to the client.

Doing Nothing

As counselors we often work harder than the couples we are attempting to stimulate to action. Several writers have indicated the pitfalls of working harder than the clients we serve (Haley, 1987; Pittman, 1987; Weeks & L'Abate, 1982). In a similar vein, Friedman (1990) noted that clients only hear when they are moving toward you, that is, when they want what you have to give. They are not likely to hear you when your words are chasing them. In a quote attributed to Murray Bowen, Friedman reported, 'If all else fails, don't just do something, stand there!' At times, we as counselors do not need to do anything. Or, stated paradoxically, we need to do nothing. Covert interventions are intended to address the dynamic that occurs when a pursuing counselor is trying to catch a fleeing couple in order to teach them something or to get a point across. As counselors we sometimes get so caught up in our task of saving and helping that we fail to notice that clients may not be seeking that which we offer. Our assumptions about being responsible lead us to simply try harder. Yet, what we often need to do at this point is to question our assumptions and in fact to do nothing.

Doing nothing might be appropriate when the couple continually disqualify the counselor by failing to complete homework assignments. Here, a symmetrical relationship would seem to develop as the counselor pushes toward change and the couple resist this movement. Selvini Palazzoli et al. (1978) suggested that the only stance left for the counselor is to change her or his position in the therapeutic relationship by declaring impotence; that is, doing nothing or indicating, 'I don't know what to do.' Selvini Palazzoli and associates, suggested that this position should be taken in a way that avoids blaming the couple and noted,

> In fact, we say that in spite of the willing collaboration of the family [couple] which has done everything possible to facilitate our understanding, we find ourselves confused and incapable of forming clear ideas, of helping them. . . . The attitude of the therapist should be neither indifferent nor overdramatic but simply that of those who dislike acknowledging their incapacity in doing what has been asked of them. (1978: 148)

It appears that it is the acknowledgment of defeat by the counselor, acknowledgment that one hasn't helped or might have been pursuing the wrong course, that moves the counseling in a new direction. If the counseling has taken on a 'yes, but' quality or if there is a period of stagnation, then most likely the tension is between the couple and the counselor. By admitting defeat and declaring confusion and a lack of knowing what to do, the counselor steps out of the power struggle with the couple and the couple can proceed with exploring their relationship.

Chip and Dale came in for counseling and presented a story of their relationship that appeared mild. These are often the types of cases in which the counselor overfunctions because she or he gets too enthused about helping the couple. Chip and Dale reported communication problems but did not report problems of substance or physical abuse nor did they have financial difficulties, nor did they appear to be involved in extramarital relationships. What they reported did not seem severe and yet they did talk about feeling hopeless in their marriage and of feeling as though the only solution was to get a divorce. We started down the path of pointing out positive aspects of their relationship and of helping them develop more effective communication. After eight sessions there was little improvement and we were aware that we were more invested in making Chip and Dale's marriage better than were they. Probably, we had made an error at the beginning of counseling by communicating in some way that we thought their marriage could be fairly easily fixed. Such an implication, even when unintended, is taken by some couples as a challenge and they proceed to show the counselor that their problems are not so simple.

At the end of the eighth session we indicated our error. We had been proceeding down the wrong path, trying to work at something that wasn't what the couple wanted. We apologized for not hearing what they had been telling us and said that they had been indicating to us all along that they wanted a divorce and we had been assuming they wanted to work on their relationship. We were sorry we had not been helpful but that now we realized their wisdom. We then proceeded to make an appointment for the following week. At the following session Chip indicated that they had a good week and that they were considering working on their marriage. They proceeded to work on important aspects of their relationship and we proceeded to follow. The change could be explained paradoxically. It would appear that it was the announcement of therapeutic impotence that moved the case in a new direction.

Weeks and L'Abate (1982) indicated that this type of doing nothing technique may be useful with clients who provide 'yes, but' responses to counselor interventions, and mentioned that they would use such a procedure as a last resort when clients are resisting movement toward change.

Summary

In this chapter, it has been noted that homework assignments to couples can clarify the intent of an intervention (overt homework) or leave the intent unclear (covert homework). When the couple's relationship demonstrates higher levels of homeostasis, reluctance to change, the counselor may find the couple returning to follow-up appointments with a litany of reasons for not completing home-work assignments such as forgetting, unexpected events occurring, and being confused as to the exact nature of the homework. In order to help the couple manage their out-of-session behavior, it was mentioned that the counselor may want to de-emphasize the intent of a homework assignment to the couple. At any rate, whether the homework assignment is more overt or covert in character, its purpose is to help the couple manage their out-of-session behavior so that they will be less likely to recycle into less fulfilling patterns of interaction. Also, as has been previously suggested, interventions presented in this chapter are only a representation of the procedures that can be used to help couples manage out-of-session behavior. The reader is encouraged to consider other interventions that more specifically meet the needs of couples on her or his caseload.

8

Therapeutic Responses to Special Issues in Counselling Couples

A number of special circumstances occur with enough frequency in couples counseling to allow the counselor to formulate alternative responses to these situations when they arise in the future. Examples of these unexpected, but not necessarily unusual, circumstances include: a request by one partner to see the counselor alone; missed appointments by either one or both members of the dyad; unscheduled phone calls; the disclosure of 'secret' information; treatment being provided by more than one service provider, etc. Not all special circumstances involve 'unexpected' elements. For example, counseling a culturally distinct couple or a couple where one partner has a diagnosed mental illness may represent special but not surprising circumstances for the counselor.

We wish that in addressing some of these special circumstances of counseling couples we could provide the most helpful way of handling the situation. Counseling, however, is not that simple and thus we will attempt to discuss some of the therapeutic issues involved in 'special circumstances' and provide alternative responses that might be helpful. The special circumstances to be discussed include: session scheduling, counselor style and authority, staging directives, and cultural issues related to counseling couples (see Figure 8.1). All these circumstances require the use of tactics and techniques that are matched to the unique therapeutic system developed between the counselor and couple.

Session Scheduling

Although weekly appointments are routine for many counselors who see couples, variations still occur and decisions need to be made with regard to scheduling. These decisions include: whom to see, how frequently to schedule, what to do when people other than those expected show up for appointments, what to do when there is a request by the couple or one of the partners for an 'extra'

Session scheduling
  Whom to see
  Frequency of appointments
  Unexpected session attendees
  Requests for individual appointments
  Clients cancel or don't show

Counselors as leaders
  Dress
  Room decor
  Phones
  Gender

Staging directives
  Conversation about change
  Defining current state as unsatisfactory
  Establishing the need for the relationship to be different
  Gaining commitment to behaving in new ways
  Providing the directive
  Blocking sabotaging of homework
  Follow-up to homework

Cultural issues
  Illustrations of cultural issues
  Cultural sensitivity and oppression
  Facilitating an understanding of diversity

Figure 8.1 *Special issues in couples counseling*

session, and what to do when clients cancel or don't show for appointments.

Whom to See

In general we prefer to see the involved couple together when we do couples counseling. This general practice may sound logical and almost ridiculous to state, at this point, yet we know a number of counselors who claim to do couples or marital counseling who never see more than one member of the dyad or never see the two members together. If one views problems and solutions as systemic in nature, that is, as lying within the relationship of the system, it seems to us that it is only reasonable to generally see the partners together. To see the couple together permits the counselor to view first hand the adaptive and maladaptive interactional patterns in the relationship. Working with the couple conjointly also permits the counselor to make direct interventions into the dyadic system, rather than trying to intervene into the couple from a distance through the efforts of only one member. Seeing the couple together permits the problem and/or solution to be defined as a couples' issue rather than as a problem of only one or the other of the partners. Finally, seeing the couple together allows the counselor to work in collaboration with the couple. That is, the counselor can work *with* the couple to address their concerns.

It is not infrequent that counselors, in initial phone calls from prospective clients, get requests from one member of a dyad to be seen individually to work on a marital issue. As with all special requests, the counselor's first thought should be about how this request to be seen individually may relate to the problem experienced by the couple. For example, the caller may want to gain or maintain control of the relationship and may believe that by coming in alone she or he can control what is said in the session and better manage what happens at home. By agreeing to the arrangement the counselor may become a part of the dysfunctionality of the system. Thus, some counselors would not honor the request. Other counselors would accept the singular arrangement, with the knowledge that in so doing they may have made an ultimately unhelpful alliance. However, their perspective may be to accept the requested arrangement for now, as a way of joining, but later to work towards getting the dyad into the session. The virtues of each approach and other approaches could be argued interminably. The critical issue is always, however, how is the counseling arrangement reflecting or challenging the dysfunctionality of the couple's relationship? How does the special circumstance posed by the couple reflect their dysfunctionality? In general, research has shown that couples counseling is more effective when both partners are seen together (see Chapter 1). However, other approaches also work at times.

Some counselors, as a standard part of their practice, see each spouse individually for at least one session. In these sessions they are making inquiry about matters that the client may be hesitant to reveal in front of their spouse. Examples of such information might include affairs that are going on, physical health problems, or a decision on the part of a spouse to end the marriage. Such information and decisions can be very powerful in influencing the course of counseling. However, once the information is revealed to the counselor, there may be both therapeutic and legal considerations. Now the client and counselor share a 'secret' and, depending on how the counselor has defined with the client her or his perspective on secrets, the counselor may have lost some power and freedom to be helpful in the relationship. Some counselors prefer not to meet separately with individual partners. They realize there may be some very powerful information that is influencing the relationship and that this information is symptomatic of the relationship. Their assumption is that the issue is a problem for the couple and that it is not helpful for the counselor to be triangled into the relationship by having an informational alliance with one member.

Another caution might be noted about counselors holding 'secret' information. Counselors need to be mindful of informing clients if one is in imminent danger. This danger could come from violence, from transmittable diseases, etc. To not pursue such information, when there is reason to have suspicion, may have legal implications for counselors. We do think that, if a decision is made to have a session with one individual, it is also helpful to see the other partner individually. This arrangement assists in keeping a balance in the relationship and helps in viewing the problem as being couple-focused rather than being the problem of one individual.

In summary, we believe it is most helpful to conduct couples counseling in a conjoint fashion. However, there are at times compelling reasons for seeing partners individually. Decisions about whom to see must always be made from the perspective of addressing the well-being of the couple as an entity and both partners.

Frequency of Appointments

Usually, almost without thinking, couples are scheduled for weekly appointments. Although weekly scheduling may be the standard practice, there are a number of situations in which deviations from this model may be helpful. Often we begin with weekly appointments of about one and one-half hours' duration. This pattern may extend for two or three weeks. The longer session time allows for more information gathering, a break if the counselor wants some quiet time to think about the session, and time to set goals and provide homework. There are two potential problems with the extended session format. If the counselor does not want the one and one-half hour format to become standard, she or he will need to express the time expectations to the couple and then enforce the time limits. Otherwise, the couple will be acculturated to expect a lengthened session. Secondly, there are some instances in which the lengthened session seems to overwhelm the couple. The couples we see often have a great deal of emotional volatility and the lengthened time to express their outrage can result in hopelessness and embarrassment that does not seem helpful to the course of counseling. Shorter sessions, in these instances, may be of assistance in establishing counseling as a safe environment.

Once goals and a direction have been established we usually move to 50-minute sessions and we often begin seeing couples every two weeks. We think that these briefer and more widely spaced sessions keep the responsibility for working on their relationship with the couple. The spacing expresses confidence that the couple can manage their relationship. We have found that with some couples weekly sessions appear to keep their relationship in a state of turbulence, that is they come in and complain about the wrongs of the week, whereas the two-week or longer spacing helps them to view their relationship over time and to not attend so much to the details.

Usually we will terminate counseling by spacing the sessions to monthly or even bi-monthly meetings. Seldom do couples gain such a great attachment to a counselor that termination is difficult. This is contrary to what seems at times to be necessary when working with individuals. In individual counseling, when a strong relationship has been established between a counselor and client, it seems that the finality of termination is an important therapeutic step in helping the client to assume responsibility for their own life. However, in couples and family counseling such dependency on the counselor is seldom a problem.

There are emergency situations when couples need to be seen more frequently but it appears more therapeutic when these exceptional situations can be minimized. First sessions are sometimes of an emergency nature. Often a critical event has occurred that has stimulated the couple to seek help. A timely response on the part of the counselor is important in capturing the change potential present in such moments. However, repeated emergency requests can provide a 'snare' (Selvini Palazzoli & Prata, 1982) in counseling if not responded to by a therapeutic move on the part of the counselor. That is, the emergency request is an acting out of the therapeutic problem and to provide an emergency response is often a move that reinforces the problem, whereas to respond in a 'nonaccommodating' manner may introduce something different into the relationship. The difference may be the confidence the counselor has that the couple can handle the problem until the next scheduled session. The difference may also be that the couple are not able to triangle a third party into their relationship the way they have in the past. There also may be important therapeutic reasons for responding in the way the couple desire to the emergency request; however, the question to be asked is, 'How does this request for an extra meeting relate to the way the couple function?'

Unexpected Session Attendees

Unless measures are taken to prevent an unexpected configuration of clients from coming to the session, the 'unexpected' will almost always occur some time during the course of counseling. Usually the unexpected configuration will be that only one member of the couple comes to the session or that the couple bring along a child. Although the appearance of only one party is probably therapeutically significant and allows the counselor to understand more about the couple, it is usually not therapeutically helpful. To some extent, the counselor may have lost her or his control and thus therapeutic leverage by letting, without giving permission, the couple determine who will be seen and when. If the counselor meets individually with the spouse, she or he will now have 'secret' information to hold with the attending partner. Although the secretness can be prevented by sharing the information with the other spouse, seeing only one of the partners still sends the implicit message that both partners are not a part of the problem or that both are not necessary for a solution.

Bringing a child or another person to the session likewise serves as a detour for counseling. However, the 'extra' member does not challenge the system perspective nor does it relieve a spouse from assuming her or his share of responsibility for the relationships. The added member will also provide an opportunity to observe the couple interacting around parenting or other interpersonal issues. While the 'extra' member will usually not prove helpful on a continuing basis, a one-time or occasional appearance can be incorporated into the counseling.

These variations in couples' attendance patterns at sessions can be minimized by establishing expectations regarding attendance early in counseling. Once the counselor has established a systems or couples view of the problem, it is relatively easy to indicate the need and expectation that both partners attend. The counselor might say something like, 'If at any time one of you cannot come to counseling, please let me know so that we can reschedule. I find that it is usually not helpful for me to meet with just one of you when we had planned to meet together.' Such a shared understanding will usually prevent the unexpected. If only one partner does come, the counselor can remind them of the understanding and reschedule the couple's session.

Requests for Individual Appointments

There are times when requests for individual appointments could be honored, and even when they are not honored, it is helpful for the counselor to provide a rationale for her or his denial that does not offend the client. Individual requests for appointments often come when the therapeutic vulnerabilities of the couple are highest, in other words at the time that the homeostasis they have developed is being most questioned. For example, a partner who suspects her or his spouse is having an affair may request an individual appointment at a time when the 'discovery' of the affair seems imminent. Or, at a time when one partner is making strong demands on the other to change, it is not unusual for the recipient of the demands to become depressed or develop a more pressing work problem that 'demands' an individual session.

Such requests provide the counselor both an opportunity to further the therapeutic gain of the couple and the danger of reaffirming old and unproductive patterns. There is no simple answer concerning the honoring of client requests for individual sessions, but in all instances the counselor should consider how the request reflects the couple's dilemma. Referring to the examples above, it may be that by meeting with the aggrieved spouse the counselor helps her or him to develop the courage and method to confront their partner. Or by meeting with the person having the affair, the counselor may assist in helping them make a decision about the continuance of the affair or how to talk with their spouse about what has gone on. The danger that the counselor must face is that she or he may become triangled in as a stress reliever in such a way that the couple avoid confronting issues of their relationships. If this scenario develops, the stability of the couple's relationship may depend on the continuance of individual sessions.

In most instances the counselor should be cautious in complying with the request for an individual session. One can usually say something like, 'I understand your wanting to see me alone, but let's talk it over at the next session and make a decision at that time.' One can then gain the time necessary to establish in one's own mind the relationship between the request and the couple's therapeutic issues. Discussing the issue in the next session also allows the couple to incorporate the request into their view of the relationship. Often, the request has lost its salience by the next appointment. If the request comes by phone, the same strategy can be used by asking the caller to call back at a specified time when the counselor will have more time and can give a response to the request. Often clients do not make the return phone call and, if they do, the counselor will be better prepared to respond to them from a therapeutic perspective (Selvini Palazzoli & Prata, 1982).

Requests for individual sessions can also be honored and used to therapeutic advantage. However, the counselor must be aware of the danger of being triangled into the couple's relationship as a stabilizing influence. To honor a request for an individual session and to use that time to help a partner to gain the courage, understandings or skills necessary to interact more productively in the system is a worthwhile venture.

Clients Cancel or Don't Show

Couples seem to cancel sessions for two reasons. Sometimes unexpected events prevent a couple from attending, for example, a child may have an accident and need attention thus forcing cancellation. Cancellations also occur because of something that is happening in counseling. Such a cancellation may occur because the counselor has proceeded too quickly and the couple sense that they are being asked to address issues in ways they do not desire. Overall, it seems to us that it is more effective if a counselor does not respond aggressively with clients who cancel. Again, the pursuit of fleeing clients is wasted energy. Usually the couple will return if the counselor takes a more patient perspective. It is helpful to affirm the wisdom of the couple's choices even if that choice seems to be premature termination. We have had a better record of keeping couples in counseling or of gaining their return to counseling by affirming their desires for time out or termination than by scolding them for ignoring the problems of their relationship.

We usually respond to occasional session cancellations by accepting the reasoning provided by the couple. If there is a discrepancy between the partners relative to the cancellation, we might make inquiry or note the discrepancy in the same manner as we would with other couple disagreements. If there are repeated cancellations we would be more likely to make inquiry about how the cancellation pattern might relate to the issues the couple is facing.

We have a greater concern when couples do not show for an appointment. Often we will wait for the couple a reasonable period of time and then make a phone call to ascertain what has happened. If the couple cannot be reached during the scheduled session period we wait a day or so to see if the couple will reinitiate contact. If they do not, we will reinitiate contact. An expression of concern by the counselor in these instances is often helpful in getting the counseling productively restarted. We do not think it is helpful for clients to terminate counseling simply by not showing up for a session. Such a 'no show' approach to termination often reflects the couple's unfinished business and lack of skill in working towards endings.

We have addressed some of the special issues counselors face with regard to session scheduling. It is our hope that counselors can more confidently and therapeutically address scheduling issues if they have thought about the issues involved in scheduling before the problems arise.

Counselors as Leaders

Counselors provide leadership to couples helping them change their thoughts, behaviors, and emotions in ways that are helpful to them. This leadership may range from being very collaborative in nature to exerting a considerable amount of authority. A number of factors: dress, therapy room decor, title, phone system, experience, age, gender and training as well as others, may all influence the counselor's ability to provide leadership.

Different couples will see the same counselor differently. The overall goal is for the counselor to use professional techniques, theory and personal style to either encourage or discourage resistance or cooperation in order to bring about therapeutic change for the couple. Young and beginning counselors often gain authority by referring to the 'science' of counseling and for instance may want to refer to the relevant literature when 'setting the stage' in prescribing homework. For example, if one member of the couple had been diagnosed as dysthymic the counselor might say, 'Research has shown that when one member of a couple is depressed the depression affects both spouses. In fact if experts don't know ahead of time which is the depressed spouse, they often are unable to identify correctly the depressed spouse even after interviewing them (Coyne, 1984). They will know depression is present but not who is depressed. The depression will have an effect on both of you. Consequently, we have found that involving both of you in treatment is more effective than seeing only one of you. So I will be asking each of you separately and the two of you together to behave in some new ways. The first thing I want you to do . . .'

An older or more experienced counselor might refer more to their own work and less to research. This counselor might say, 'I have treated over the past dozen years about 300 couples in which one of the couples was depressed and I have found that if we . . .' In both instances the counselor is making a clinical judgment about how one needs to present oneself and information in order to have an optimal impact on the couple. Some counselors find 'one down' positions to be helpful in gaining client cooperation. They allow the couple to help them and thus avoid resistance that is produced by more authoritarian approaches. For example, a young counselor in working with an older couple might say, 'Now, I haven't been married nearly as long as you and I haven't seen nearly as much as you've seen, so if you notice me missing some things that are important to you call it to my attention. Allright?' A more collaborative or joint problem-solving approach frequently promotes a cooperative couple–counselor relationship.

There is no one right answer concerning the presentation of self or therapeutic strategies to be used in working with all couples. Rather the issues and approaches lie within the therapeutic system. Different counselors because of gender, age, interpersonal style, and skill have differing therapeutic relationships with clients. The following are some of the issues counselors consider when working to establish a therapeutic atmosphere. These factors impact not only the session but also the leadership the counselor can give to couples between sessions.

Dress

We assume that most couples view the counselor as a professional and, at least for initial interviews, when one is attempting to establish a working atmosphere, it is usually helpful to dress in a manner consistent with professional dress in the geographical area in which one works. Again, age may be a factor in choosing the degree of formality of dress. In our experience it seems that 'younger' counselors have a bit more credibility at least with 'older' clients if they dress in a more formal manner, whereas, for most couples, it seems that an appearance of age in the counselor creates an atmosphere of authority that reduces the need to gain authority through dress.

Room Decor

In considering decor, it seems the most common consideration of counselors in working with couples is the presence of membership certificates, licenses, awards, and family pictures. In some locales the display of certificates, licenses, and disclosure statements may be a legal matter as well as a matter of therapeutic impact. All of these items may be viewed by clients as statements of expertise and/or the nature and identity of the counselor. For example, to have an award on the wall from a domestic violence center may send a protective message to some clients and a threatening message to others. Family pictures may denote valid experience to some clients while others may see such pictures as a sign that the counselor opposes divorce and that they cannot talk about their greatest concerns. If a couple or a spouse seems to be especially interested in credentials one might choose three courses of action. One could ignore their interest, respond to their interest by explaining credentials fully, or inquire concerning their interest. Each of these responses will have a differing impact on the influence the counselor has in the relationship. The response the counselor chooses will depend on what she or he considers to be the most therapeutic for the couple. Certainly, there is no one right way to decorate an office but office decor does have at least an initial impact on the couple's view of the counselor.

Phones
With regard to phones and authority there are issues of both a technological and professional nature. Counselors often decide between answering the phone themselves, using a secretary and/or using an answering machine. The method one chooses to use may be governed by time and financial constraints. That is, the financial resources available to a practice may determine the phone system and answering service used. However, to be aware of the therapeutic impact of each of these approaches is important. For example, clients have differing reactions if they speak to the counselor, to a secretary, or to an answering machine. To use the communication system to its greatest advantage may be crucial in retaining clients and in influencing their therapeutic gain. It is important to remember that the counselor's authority and power begins when she or he says 'hello.' If an answering machine is used an invitational statement must be developed as a lead so that clients will leave messages. Such recorded statements as well as comments given directly over the phone are usually subject to legal control by licensing bodies or ethical sanctions by professional organizations.

Gender
The gender of the counselor interacting with the gender perceptions of the clients is also influential in the process of establishing and maintaining leadership and therapeutic direction. Often it seems that greater latitude of counselor behavior can take place between counselors and spouses of the same gender while a narrower range of behavior is available when a counselor is working across gender. Certainly the above depiction is not always true but it does seem to have merit as a generalization. The issue of latitude of counselor behavior is important in being able to initiate new behavior and in being able to destabilize the current dynamics of the couple. For example, if the counseling decision is to destabilize by confrontation, it seems that the confrontation is often more effective if it takes place between a counselor and client of the same gender.

Brian and Jodie had been seen for six sessions and had made little progress. Brian was feeling highly criticized by Jodie and was voicing a desire to end the relationship. Typically a counselor will have little success in confronting a spouse who wants to end a relationship. Usually, it seems that time is better spent empowering the 'victim' to be more confrontive, to get in touch with their own dissatisfaction in the relationship, and to develop their own interests and strengths. However, because neither party in the relationship had made much effort to change and because the counselor was a male we asked the counselor to indicate to the male spouse that many of the problems of the marriage were his fault. The counselor also indicated to him that, if he wanted to keep his spouse, he would have to work very hard to court her and regain her interest. The result was that the wife was empowered, she felt supported, and became more assertive. Although the husband had expressed a desire to end the relationship, he responded to his wife's new sense of strength by becoming more attentive.

Although from a systems perspective we know that the fault in a marriage does not lie just with one spouse, we used the strategy of blaming one spouse as a way of unbalancing the marriage. Our guiding principle was that, given the magnitude of the confrontation, it would be more effective for the confrontation to take place, at least overtly, between the counselor and the client of the same gender. Cross-gender confrontation will often triangle the counselor in such a way that the issues of counseling are between the counselor and the opposite gender spouse rather than within the couple's relationship.

Staging Directives

When a counselor prescribes behavior for a couple to perform while a session is in progress, she or he can correct the couple's perceptions and interactions instantly. However, no comparable corrections are available for making adjustments in a couple's behavior once they leave the session. It is therefore important to 'get the homework right' the first time. The issues to be considered in 'getting it right' include the couple's level of motivation and their belief that change will take place, the counselor's confidence in the usefulness and importance of the homework, the tone of the delivery of the homework and, finally, the content and process of the directive itself.

The discovery of the pattern of the couple's problem, that is, the behaviors that maintain the problem, is an essential task of the counselor. Over time the counselor develops a repertoire of interventions that she or he employs when a pattern of behavior is discovered. At the point of pattern discovery the counselor reviews her or his repertoire of interventions and, with modifications to fit the circumstances of the couple in the room, 'plays' one of the rehearsed interventions. One of the preparation phases in staging a directive is to assist the couple in anticipating change in their relationship.

Conversation about Change

Counselors have to assume at least some of the responsibility of helping their clients become motivated to change. In many of his workshops, Jay Haley discusses how therapists can assume partial responsibility for change by having ways of talking about change that intrigue, excite, and challenge the couple to participate in the process of change. When couples have confidence that the counselor has their best interest at heart and when they believe change will occur and that the change will be helpful they are more willing to follow a directive. Thus it is important to have several ways of asking questions and talking about change and enough to say so that 15–20 minutes can be occupied helping the couple to build a sense of positive anticipation. The following are some counseling leads that provide a flavor of the ideas that might create an environment for change with couples.

- It is really hard to commit yourself to change because to do so makes you feel like you are saying you are committed to the marriage and that is frightening. It might make more sense to commit yourself to seeing how good you can make the marriage. Whether or not you stay married will depend on how good your marriage is. Are you willing to see how good you can make your relationship?
- I always find change interesting. For me, change is like going around a sharp corner in the car. I'm sailing along enjoying the scenery and suddenly I come to a sharp curve. I'm never quite prepared and it seems I'm a little out-of-control. It's exciting and yet frightening. I can't quite make out what is going by the window. I have to watch for other drivers, make sure I stay on the road and look under control to whoever else is in the car. I can't turn back and sometimes I can't even slow down much. Then I make it around the corner, the view is nice again and what went on while I was rounding the bend comes into focus.

- Well it is Spring (or you're about to turn 40, or school is starting, or it's winter and life slows down, or there are any number of reasons to consider changing) and so it seems like a good time to change.
- Would you prefer the change to be fast or slow? Do you think fast change is more helpful to you or is slow change more helpful (Haley, 1987)?
- How do you think the changes you want in your relationship will take place?
- When it comes time to change most couples have a difficult time making a commitment. They think their relationship is so bad that the change will have to be enormous. My experience is that sometimes only a small change is needed, and sometimes a small change makes a big difference.
- If this problem of _____ were to be solved, what would each of you be doing so differently?
- It's really difficult to commit yourself to change, because you've felt so much hurt before. You may want to go slow.

Conversations about change are part of the directive-staging process that includes: helping the couple to announce that the way their life is progressing is not satisfactory; establishing that they would like their relationship to be different; gaining their commitment to behave in new ways; providing the directive; exposing the behavior the couple might use to render the directive ineffective; and following up on the directive and adjusting the process. The following are some ideas that may be adapted in helping clients through the change process.

Defining Current State as Unsatisfactory

An initial task in helping a couple to change often involves helping them to announce that their relationship is not satisfactory and thus there is a need for change. When couples come for counseling, it is implicit that there are difficulties in their relationship, however it is not unusual for one member to deny the presence of a problem. It is also quite typical for couples to come with serious complaints and yet fail to recognize that they have a relationship problem. Recognition by the couple of their concern is often a significant aspect of their becoming serious about finding solutions or setting goals for counseling. Illustrative quotations are provided that may be helpful in moving a couple toward problem recognition and ownership. The latter examples might be used when couples have trouble acknowledging these difficulties.

- I'm not sure that each of you even believes there is a problem in your relationship. What do you think?
- What do each of you see as being a concern/problem in your relationship/marriage?
- What do the two of you, together, see as a problem/concern in your relationship?
- You both talk about a lot of pain and unhappiness right now, but not much about those things that are going well for you. That's pretty typical when couples first come to counseling. You both think there are some issues you need to work on?
- Fred, you talk of your unhappiness with Jane. She works too much, never spends time with you and spends too much time with friends and family. Yet, Jane, it seems you are happy in the relationship. Your only concern is about how unhappy Fred is. I have an idea about what might be going on. Do you want to know what I think? (Usually, it is helpful if the couple ask the counselor for her or his ideas.) I think, Jane, you too might be unhappy about some things, you've mentioned feeling stretched, tired and so on, but you seem to fear that if you really share your concerns Fred will either say 'Let's get a divorce' or tell you to cut back your work. Is that right?
- Sharing your problems/concerns seems to be a problem for the two of you.
- You each say that there is a problem in your relationship, but I'm not sure you really think that you are a part of the problem.
- If you didn't have this problem of _____ in your relationship, what would be different?
- If you were just to imagine what a possible problem in your marriage looked like, what would it be?
- Who is your best friend? What would she or he say if I were to mention, 'You know Fred and Jane are having some problems in their marriage, what do you think are their problems?' After the problem is reported, the counselor can say, 'Is that a problem for you?'

Establishing the Need for the Relationship
to be Different

Couples who acknowledge that they have problems in their relationship or even that their relationship is in trouble may still have a difficult time indicating that they want their life together to be different. Often this hesitancy may come from a feeling of impotence about making life better, a fear that if they risk making a change they also risk being hurt, or a fear that if they get more involved with their spouse they will feel even more anger and sadness about their relationship. Yet, it often seems the acknowledgment of a desire for the relationship to be different is a step in the change process. Even to say, 'I want our relationship to be different' is to affirm the other person as a partner. Such an affirmation can be quite encouraging. For a counselor to initiate a change process without recognition by the couple that change is desired can lead to resistance and frustrations. The following counseling leads are sometimes useful in helping the couple to establish a desire for a different relationship.

- Do you each want things to be different?
- Change is frightening, but what do you think will happen if you don't change? (*Couple respond.*) Yes, and then what would happen?
- You folks sure seem stuck and yet I'm not sure you want to change/I'm not sure things are bad enough to change.
- Do you want to know what I think? I think you get something out of this fighting (problem behavior). It's like you really want to be close and this is the only way you know how. What do you think? Do you want to find some other ways of being close?
- If your relationship was going well right now what would be different? What would you be looking forward to?
- Let's see, Fred and Jane, you were married about ____ years ago. When you look back to that time, what did you think would be going on in your marriage now? Does that dream you had then seem realistic? When things are better for you again, what do you think you will be looking forward to in five years?
- Sometimes it is real hard to say you want things to be different because you feel so hopeless that you're not sure they can be different. (Empathic responses may result in further discussion of the couple's relationship and further hope for change.)

Some of the above statements attempt to establish positive motivations for current behavior, for example fighting helps you to be close, while others help to establish an expectancy of positive change, such as when things are better for you again. All of these comments are intended to help couples in announcing the need for change in their relationship.

Gaining Commitment to Behaving in New Ways
Homework may range from a counselor–couple planned activity to a counselor suggestion to a counselor request to an assignment

required by the counselor. For some couples jointly planned activities or suggestions may be all that is needed. For others, requiring their commitment to engage in the homework may be needed even before the homework is prescribed. In all instances careful consideration must be given to the strategy used to help couples behave in new ways. The following leads provide examples that set the stage for making a commitment to change and these examples range from collaborating to making a suggestion to requesting a change to requiring a change.

- What do you think you could do to make things better? (Collaboration)
- Let's discuss some things you could do to make your relationship better. (Collaboration)
- You each have a lot of complaints, but I'm not sure, it doesn't sound like you are quite ready to do something different (change) yet. What do you think? What do you think, Fred, are you ready to make some changes? What about you, Jane? (Collaboration)
- Could you tolerate it if things got better, I don't know? (Collaboration)
- You know all couples have tensions or problems in their relationship but the difference between satisfied or fulfilled couples and those who are not is the ability to solve or work through these difficulties. With this in mind, I might suggest that you consider _____. (Suggestion)
- You know, I thought about giving this to you to do last week, but it didn't seem quite right then. However, I think you're now ready. I'd like you to consider _____. (Suggestion)
- I'm not saying you have to do this, but this week you may want to _____. Of course, you may also choose not to do this. (Suggestion)
- This week I want you to _____, okay? (Request)
- I have something for you to do that I think will be helpful. It may not, that's really up to you. But, you have to agree to do it before I'll tell you what it is. Okay? (Requirement) (If the couple agree 'too quickly' the counselor may want to reinforce the assignment by saying, 'You may want to think about that a bit more. Do you still want to do it? So, Jane, you've agreed and, Fred, you've agreed?) (Adapted from Watzlawick, Weakland, & Fisch, 1974.)

Providing the Directive
As discussed in Chapter 7, the prescription of homework usually follows one of two paths. The prescription can be overt, in which

case the directions, given clearly, relate to the ends desired and the couple have a shared perception with each other and the counselor about how the activity relates to the goal. Prescriptions can also be covert, in which case the counselor does not share the objective of the prescribed behavior with the couple. In reality most homework has both overt and covert aspects. At least the impact of the homework often goes beyond that anticipated by either the counselor or the couple.

Blocking Sabotaging of Homework

The anticipation of how a couple might resist homework is important to ensuring that the activity has the intended effect. Couples can often be inoculated against 'spoiling' the homework by discussing the techniques they might use to sabotage the activity (Haley, 1987). The discussion may take place by asking the couple what might go wrong and by the counselor speculating about how the couple might sabotage the action. The following counselor leads illustrate how this inoculating against the sabotaging of homework might be conducted.

- If you were going to do something so that this homework didn't work/wasn't helpful, what would you do? What else could you do to prevent the homework from being effective?
- Do you know/want to know what I think you might do in order to mess this up? I think you might _____ or _____.
- I don't think it would be helpful for you to get better too quickly, you may still need this problem.
- I don't think this homework will necessarily make your relationship better but I think you will be able to learn some important things about yourselves if you do it.

Follow-up to Homework

It is important for counselors to follow up on their homework assignments to couples. If there is no follow-up, a message is conveyed that the assignment was really not very important (Haley, 1987). It is helpful for the counselor to write a case note each time homework is given as a reminder for follow-up in the next session. Some counselors even write their homework on duplicate prescription pads so that they and the couple have a copy (Hudson & O'Hanlon, 1991). Overt homework can be followed up with direct questioning. Did the activity have the desired outcome? A more vague approach to following up covert homework is usually indicated. Example questions include: What happened as a result of the homework? What did the couple learn? The counselor should show interest in the outcome but not indicate interest in whether a particular objective has been achieved. Remember, covert homework is trying to address resistance to change and too much interest in change at the follow-up defeats the intent of the covert assignment.

Finally, the counselor needs to have a strategy for working with the couple when the homework was not completed. Usually, it is most helpful for the counselor to assume the responsibility for why the homework was not completed. Occasionally, though, it is more helpful to take a punitive approach toward the couple when the homework was not attempted or completed. Haley (1987) made a similar comment about following up on homework assignments that are not completed and mentioned how one can respond in a 'nice way' or a 'not-so-nice' way. The counselor might signal assumption of responsibility for failed homework by indicating that she or he did not provide clear instructions about the homework. Another approach is to indicate that the homework must not have met the needs of the couple at the time. The counselor might also mention that she or he had erred in not making clear the purpose of the homework and, thus, it is understandable why the couple had not completed the assignment. All of these responses are designed to minimize tension between the counselor and couple and relieve any sense of blame or guilt the couple might experience. In each instance the groundwork is established for prescribing the previous homework or for prescribing new homework. The counselor can provide clearer instructions, establish a better connection between the directive and the goals of counseling or indicate why now the time is right for the homework. Although it is most often advantageous to the goals of counseling for the counselor to assume the responsibility for a couple's failure to undertake or complete a homework assignment, there are times when responsibility for failed homework should fall on the clients.

Those times when one might take a more punitive approach toward failed homework involve clinical judgments relative to how best to stimulate the couple to work. One might take an approach as suggested by Haley (1987) and say something like,

- I'm sorry to hear that you didn't complete the assignment. That is an opportunity lost, a chance that you will never have again. I think that assignment would have really enlightened you about your relationship and made quite a difference. That is too bad.
- That's too bad. I thought you were at the point where what I

indicated for you to do would have really made a difference. Well, we can't cry over spilled milk, that moment is gone.

When these latter homework follow-ups are used with clients it seems that the likelihood of their completing future assignments is increased. Paradoxically, some couples will make gains after being scolded for not completing homework. It is as though they are showing the counselor that they can get better without doing the work. The staging both before a directive is given and after the couple have completed the assignment is critical to the success of the homework. At times it seems the enticement and stimulation of the staging are more important than the directive. The directive clearly loses its impact if approaches are not taken to ensure completion.

Cultural Issues in Couples Counseling

Depending on the definitions one uses of culture, all issues in couples counseling could be viewed as tensions resulting from cultural diversity. From a cultural perspective one develops values, thoughts, behaviors, and expectations by interacting in a socio-cultural context. The context includes many variables: race, ethnicity, gender, education, economics, religion, etc. Within these contexts are developed dynamic world views of how life does and should operate. Couple problems then can be conceptualized as a clash of culturally derived world views. These cultural world view clashes may occur for the couple over issues of childrearing, how money is earned or spent, household chores, uses of alcohol or other substances, eating habits, relationships with extended family members, etc. The clashes are bound only by the phenomena of life to which the couple attach meaning.

Illustrations of Cultural Issues

The multicultural perspective to counseling is seen as a Fourth Force in Counseling (Pederson, 1991), a way of viewing all counseling issues. Although we did not choose a multicultural lens as the context for writing this book, we do believe a multicultural perspective to be extremely helpful when engaging in couples counseling. In some ways every counseling encounter, every couples counseling session is multicultural in some aspect and thus multicultural counseling skills are essential and unavoidable. From a multicultural perspective counselors need to attend to those tensions that occur between partners, between a couple or one of the partners and other social systems, and between the couple or a partner and the counselor. Tensions can be seen as a lack of world view fit. When these differences can be discussed as cultural then two people can disagree without one being right or the other wrong because the differences start from culturally different assumptions.

> For example, we recently worked with a couple in which the husband, Mike, an African American, was being highly criticized by his wife Pam, a Caucasian. The criticism appeared to be aimed at getting Mike to decrease his workload and stop allowing his bosses to take advantage of him by making him do their work. Mike's assumption was that as a black male he could retain his job and entertain even a remote chance of advancement only by pleasing his bosses and making life as easy for them as possible. Pam thought that Mike's work style lacked dignity and reflected poorly on him as a man. When it was shown that both views were culturally based, a more accommodating view developed between the couple. Mike engaged in reality testing behavior to see whether his view of the tenuousness of his work situation was correct and Pam became more supportive of Mike's approach to work. The views of both Pam and Mike had a cultural basis. The exploration of their world view regarding gender, race, and work was a step in the development of new views that valued the relationship, promoted understanding, and set new boundaries.

Cultural Sensitivity and Oppression

The need for cultural sensitivity is frequently related to the experience of oppression by one or both partners in a relationship. Oppression is used here rather generally as a system in which access to services, rewards, the making of decisions, privileges, and participation in family or societal activity is based on membership in a particular group. Typical areas of cultural oppression include: religion, age, racial/ethnic heritage, disability, sex, and gender orientation (Myers et al., 1991; Reynolds & Pope, 1991). Breunlin, Schwartz, and MacKune-Karrer (1992) add education, regional background, and immigration–acculturation as cultural areas to which counselors need to be sensitive. These areas of diversity are often not discrete phenomena of which only one type of oppression can be experienced by an individual. Rather individuals and couples may experience multiple identities and oppressions (Reynolds & Pope, 1991). For example, an aging, ethnic-minority, disabled male would have multiple identities and may experience multiple oppressions. A racially mixed couple will experience oppression because of their racial backgrounds and the woman, regardless of race, will usually experience oppression. Thus, counselors need to be sensitive to the multiple cultural identities and oppressions their clients experience.

Facilitating an Understanding of Diversity

In thinking about issues of cultural diversity as they relate to couples the counselor might consider the following questions:

- What is the fit between the counselor and the couple's sociocultural contexts: disabling conditions, religion, age, social/ethnic heritage, sex, gender orientation, economic status, education, regional background, and immigration status?
- What is the fit between the partners relative to the noted cultural variables?
- What is the fit between the partners and both extended families?
- What is the fit between partners individually and as a couple and the environments in which they live and work?
- Have there been major changes on cultural variables for the couple in the distant or recent past, for example, an onset of a disabling condition, a change of religious affiliation?
- Do the couple view their cultural differences as a liability or an opportunity?

As counselors, we can become overwhelmed with the amount of cultural knowledge and sensitivity that is helpful in working with couples. We realize that even though we continually work to strengthen our sensitivity and knowledge it often seems that an attitude of (respect) and (humbleness) about differences and a curiosity about people and their cultures are our best tools in negotiating multicultural encounters.

Summary

The focus of this chapter has been largely on formulating therapeutic responses to special issues in counseling couples. We could have discussed an array of the special problems that one sees in counseling couples, such as sexual, substance abuse, depression, grief, physical and emotional abuse, etc. Knowledge of such problems is important and yet it is not possible to be knowledgeable about a wide array of problems. The counselor's specialization lies not in the content areas but rather in areas of process and change. The task of the counselor is to be what Friedman (1986) calls a nonanxious presence in the system that provides and supports leadership in ways so that direction can be taken. Thus we have discussed alternative responses a counselor might use in providing leadership to some of the 'special' process issues encountered in counseling couples.

Epilogue: Thoughts along the Way

To engage in the writing process is to be involved in a life-changing adventure; perhaps that is why journaling is so often recommended to clients. It seems that writing challenges us to observe our counseling more closely and the observation produces an evolving set of ideas that cycle back into the practice and subsequent observations. This venture in writing has helped us to clarify and affirm some of our thoughts about working with couples. In thinking about our practice, we have seen some new ideas emerge and we have changed some of the things we do in counseling.

The ideas about motivation, comprehension, and management provide an interrelated set of constructs that are important to all counseling endeavors. Couples who report success in their relationships are challenged to have a coordinated and mutually fulfilling life together. They are motivated to accommodate to each other so they can decipher areas of life in which they can engage each other and areas in which they need to avoid such engagement. Couples who perceive themselves as successful also seem to have developed a set of meanings for their relationship that stabilize them in the present and guide them into the future. Couples who seem to experience undue tension in their lives appear to have comprehension and meaning systems that attribute negative intent to their partner; that blame their partner and do not focus on self-contribution. Such a self-focus often fails to accommodate to the other's perspective. Relationship skills are also an important part of a couple's subsystem, although the skill development required to maintain a satisfactory relationship may vary from couple to couple. Some couples are involved in more complex relationships than others and thus require more behavioral skills to negotiate their relationships. Issues that add to complexity in couple relationships include: dual careers, stepfamilies, divorce, geographically distant relationships, etc. Some couples also have higher expectations of their relationships and, consequently, of their relationship skills, than do other couples.

The growth we have experienced, as counselors, relative to the areas of motivation, comprehension and management, has come primarily in the comprehension area but the reverberations impact motivation and management. From one perspective, couples counseling can be seen as a task of 'doing' and 'viewing' (O'Hanlon & Weiner-Davis, 1989). Counselors are helping couples to behave differently in their relationship and they are helping them to view that is, to understand, conceptualize, and comprehend their relationship differently. When couples behave differently they solve problems and when they understand their relationship differently problems are often dissolved (Andersen, 1991). The former 'problem-solving approaches' hold the premise that if a relationship problem can be defined in behavioral terms then behaving differently offers the possibility of a solution. The assumption in the 'viewing approach' is that we may create the problem by the language we use to describe the problem. The problem is contained in how we think. Consequently, if we would conceptualize the situation differently the problem might disappear. This is a constructivist perspective espoused by Gergen and Kaye (1992), Andersen (1991), and White and Epston (1990). Reframing and relabeling are techniques that frequently allow a couple to see circumstances from a new perspective that in turn allows them to experience a subsequent diminishing of symptoms. An impetus for the heightened importance of understanding and conceptualization in couple relationships is the diversity that we are experiencing in our society. Couples come to their relationship from diverse spaces – worlds of work, cultural and racial backgrounds, family experiences. This diversity must be accommodated and appreciated in couple relationships. Thus useful meaning systems, understandings, and stories must be developed that assist couples in coordinating and finding satisfaction in their lives amidst the diversity with which they live.

This attention to conceptualizations and meaning systems has resulted in the development of 'meaning-making techniques.' Some of the more traditional methods of 'meaning making' include metaphor creation, reframing, relabeling and circular questioning. Recently, the practice of creating meanings that allow couples to select and develop stories about their lives has been strengthened by the work of Tom Andersen (1991) and his associates, who use reflecting teams as a way of creating meanings germane to the difficulties couples experience. Michael White and David Epston (1990) likewise have developed means, primarily narrative, that help couples to externalize their problems and gain control in developing revised stories about their lives and their life together. From a counseling technique perspective our growth area is in the development and integration of methods of 'meaning making' in couple relationships. However, whether in the area of comprehension, motivation or management, we hope our efforts will assist others in continuing their journey of improving their skills in working with couples.

References

Adler, A. (1964) *Social interest: A challenge to mankind*. New York: Caprion Books.

American Psychiatric Association (1987) *Diagnostic and Statistical Manual of Mental Disorders*, Third Edition, Revised. Washington, DC: American Psychiatric Association.

Andersen, T., (1991) 'The context and history of the reflecting team,' in T. Andersen (ed.), *The reflecting team: Dialogues and dialogues about the dialogues*. New York: W.W. Norton. pp. 3-14.

Anderson, C.M., & Stewart, S. (1983) *Mastering resistance: A practical guide to family therapy*. New York: Guilford.

Andolfi, M. (1980) 'Prescribing the families' own dysfunctional rules as a therapeutic strategy,' *Journal of Marital and Family Therapy*, 6: 29-36.

Andolfi, M., Angelo, C., Menghi, P., & Nicolo-Corigliano, A. (1983) *Behind the family mask*. New York: Brunner/Mazel.

Ansbacher, H.L., & Ansbacher, R.R. (1956) *The individual psychology of Alfred Adler: A systematic presentation in selections from his writings*. New York: Harper & Row.

Antonovsky, A. (1979) *Health, stress, and coping: New perspectives on mental and physical well-being*. San Francisco: Jossey-Bass.

Antonovsky, A. (1987) *Unraveling the mystery of health: How people manage stress and stay well*. San Francisco, CA: Jossey-Bass.

Barker, P. (1985) *Using metaphors in psychotherapy*. New York: Brunner/Mazel.

Beavers, R.W., & Kaslow, F.W. (1981) 'The anatomy of hope', *Journal of Marital and Family Therapy*, 7: 119-26.

Bowen, M. (1978) *Family therapy in clinical practice*. New York: Jason Aronson.

Breunlin, D.C., Schwartz, R.C., & MacKune-Karrer, B. (1992) *Meta frameworks: Transcending the models of family therapy*. San Francisco: Jossey-Bass.

Bubenzer, D.L., Zimpfer, D., & Mahrle, C. (1990) [Community counselors reporting of categories of client problems]. Unpublished raw data.

Bubenzer, D.L., West, J.D., Detrude, J., Mahrle, C.L., & Sand-Pringle, C. (1991) 'Prescriptive metaphor creation for individual, couple, and family therapy,' *Individual Psychology: The Journal of Adlerian Theory, Research & Practice*, 47(2): 272-9.

Bulman, R., & Wortman, C.B. (1977) 'Attributions of blame and coping in the "real world": Severe accident victims react to their lot,' *Journal of Personality and Social Psychology*, 35: 351-63.

Campbell, J. (1988) (Interview by Bill Moyers) *Joseph Campbell and the power of myth*. (Cassette Recording No. A101). Montauk, NY: Mystic Fire Video.

Coyne, J.C. (1984) 'Strategic therapy with depressed married persons: Initial agenda, themes and interventions,' *Journal of Marital and Family Therapy*. 10: 53-62.

de Shazer, S. (1985) *Keys to solution in brief therapy*. New York: W.W. Norton.

de Shazer, S. (1988) *Clues: Investigating solutions in brief therapy*. New York: W.W. Norton.

Dattilio, F.M., & Padesky, C.A. (1990) *Cognitive therapy with couples*. Sarasota, FL: Professional Resource Exchange.

Derogatis, L.R. (1977) *SCL-90-R: Administration, scoring, and procedures manual II*. Towson, MD: Clinical Psychomatic Research.

Dodson, L.S. & Kurpius, D. (1977) *Family counseling: A systems approach*. Muncie, IN: Accelerated Development.

Ducette, J., & Keane, A. (1984) 'Why me? An attributional analysis of a major illness,' *Research in Nursing and Health*, 7: 257–64.

Fisch, R., Weakland, J.H., & Segal, L. (1982) *The tactics of change: Doing therapy briefly*. San Francisco: Jossey-Bass.

Friedman, E. (1986) 'Resources for healing and survival in families,' in M.A. Karpel (ed.), *Family resources: The hidden partner in family therapy*. New York: Guilford. pp. 65–115.

Friedman, E. (1990) *Friedman's fables*. New York: Guilford.

Geiss, S.K., & O'Leary, K.D. (1981) 'Therapist ratings of frequency and severity of marital problems: Implications for research,' *Journal of Marital and Family Therapy*, 10: 515–20.

Gergen, K.J., & Kaye, J. (1992) 'Beyond narrative in the negotiation of therapeutic meaning,' in S. McNamee & K.J. Gergen (eds.) *Therapy as social construction*. London: Sage. pp. 166–85.

Glick, P.C., & Spanier, G.B. (1980) 'Married and unmarried cohabitation in the United States,' *Journal of Marriage and the Family*, 42, 19–30.

Goldenberg, I., & Goldenberg, H. (1980) *Family therapy: An overview*. Belmont, CA: Wadsworth, Inc.

Goldenberg, I., & Goldenberg, H. (1990) *Counseling today's families*. Pacific Grove, CA: Brooks/Cole.

Gordon, D. (1978) *Therapeutic metaphors*. Cupertino, CA: META Publications.

Gottman, J.M. (1979) *Marital interaction: Experimental investigations*. New York: Academic Press.

Guerin, P.J., & Pendagast, E.G. (1976) 'Evaluation of family system and genogram,' in P.J. Guerin (ed.), *Family Therapy*. New York: Gardner. pp. 450–64.

Guerin, P.J., Fay, L.F., Burden, S.L., & Kautto, J.G. (1987) *The evaluation and treatment of marital conflict: A four-stage approach*. New York: Basic Books.

Gurman, A.S., Kniskern, D.P., & Pinsof, W.M. (1986) 'Research on marital and family therapies,' in S.L. Garfield & A.E. Bergin (eds), *Handbook of psychotherapy and behavior change*. New York: John Wiley & Sons. pp. 565–624.

Hacker, A. (ed.) (1983) *U/S: A statistical portrait of the American people*. New York: Viking Press.

Haley, J. (1963) *Strategies of psychotherapy*. New York: Grune & Stratton.

Haley, J. (1973) *Uncommon therapy: The psychiatric techniques of Milton Erickson, M.D.* New York: Norton.

Haley, J. (1976) *Problem solving therapy*. San Francisco: Jossey-Bass.

Haley, J. (1984) *Ordeal therapy*. San Francisco: Jossey-Bass.

Haley, J. (1987) *Problem solving therapy.* (2nd ed.) San Francisco: Jossey-Bass.

Haley, J. (1990) 'Why not long-term therapy?' in J.K. Zeig & S.G. Gilligan (eds) *Brief therapy: Myths, methods, and metaphors.* New York: Brunner/Mazel. pp. 3–17.

Hudson, P., & O'Hanlon, W. (1991) *Rewriting love stories: Brief marital therapy.* New York: W.W. Norton.

Imber-Black, E., Roberts, J., & Whiting, R. (1988) *Rituals in families and family therapy.* New York: Norton.

Knox, D. (1971) *Marriage happiness.* Champaign, IL: Research Press.

Kobasa, S.C. (1979) 'Stressful life events, personality, and health: An inquiry into hardiness,' *Journal of Personality and Social Psychology*, 37: 1–11.

Kohlberg, L. (1971) 'From is to ought: How to commit the naturalistic fallacy and get away with it in the study of moral development,' in T. Mischel (ed.), *Cognitive development and epistemology.* New York: Academic Press.

Landfield, A.W., & Rivers, P.C. (1975) 'An introduction to interpersonal transaction and rotating dyads,' *Psychotherapy: Theory, Research and Practice*, 12: 365–73.

Lankton, S. & Lankton, C. (1983) *The answer within: a clinical framework of Ericksonian hypnotherapy.* New York: Brunner/Mazel.

Lauer, R.H., & Lauer, J.C. (1991) *Marriage and family: The quest for intimacy.* Dubuque, IA: Wm. C. Brown.

Lederer, W.J., & Jackson, D.D. (1968) *The mirages of marriage.* New York: W.W. Norton.

McGoldrick, M., & Gerson, R. (1985) *Genograms in family assessment.* New York: W.W. Norton.

Madanes, C. (1981) *Strategic family therapy.* San Francisco: Jossey-Bass.

Markman, H.J. (1981) 'Prediction of marital distress: A 5-year follow-up,' *Journal of Consulting and Clinical Psychology*, 49: 760–2.

Markman, H.J., Floyd, S., Stanley, S., & Storasli, R. (1988) 'The prevention of marital distress: A longitudinal investigation,' *Journal of Consulting and Clinical Psychology*, 56: 210–17.

Miller, J.F., & Powers, M.J. (1988) 'Development of an instrument to measure hope,' *Nursing Research*, 1: 6–10.

Minuchin, S. (1974) *Families and family therapy.* Cambridge, MA: Harvard University Press.

Minuchin, S., & Fishman, H.C. (1981) *Family therapy techniques.* Cambridge, MA: Harvard University Press.

Monte, E.P. (1989) 'The relationship life-cycle,' in G.R. Wecks (ed.) *Treating couples: The intersystem model of the Marriage Council of Philadelphia.* New York: Brunner/Mazel. pp. 287–316.

Mosak, H., & Dreikurs, R. (1973) 'Adlerian psychotherapy,' in R. Corsini (ed.), *Current psychotherapies.* Itasca, IL: F.E. Peacock. pp. 35–83.

Myers, L.J., Speight, S.L., Highlen, P.S., Cox, C.I., Reynolds, A.L., Adams, E.M., & Hanley, C.P. (1991) 'Identity development and worldview: Toward an optimal conceptualization,' *Journal of Counseling and Development*, 70: 54–63.

National Center for Health Statistics (1988) *Monthly vital statistics report.* (DHHS Publication No. PHS 88-1120) Hyattsville, MD: Public Health Service.

Nichols, M. (1984) *Family therapy: Concepts and methods.* New York: Gardner.

O'Hanlon, W.H., & Weiner-Davis, M. (1989) *In search of solutions: A new direction in psychotherapy*. New York: W.W. Norton.

Office of Population Censuses and Surveys (OCPS) (1991) *General Household Survey 1989*. London: HMSO.

Papp, P. (1976) 'Family choreography,' in P. Guerin (ed.), *Family therapy, theory and practice*. New York: Gardner. pp. 465-79.

Papp, P. (1981) 'Paradoxes,' in S. Minuchin, & H.C. Fishman (eds), *Family therapy techniques*. Cambridge, MA: Harvard University Press. pp. 244-61.

Pederson, P.B. (1991) 'Introduction to the special issue on multiculturalism as a fourth force in counseling,' *Journal of Counseling and Development*, 70: 4.

Pelletier, K.R. (1981) *Longevity: Fulfilling our biological potential*. New York: Delacorte Press/Seymour Lawrence.

Piercy, F. (1983) 'A game for interrupting coercive marital interaction,' *Journal of Marital and Family Therapy*, 4: 435-6.

Piercy, F. (1991, October) 'A family therapy model: Short circuiting marital arguments.' Workshop presented to the Counseling and Human Development Services Program, Kent State University, Kent, OH.

Pittman, F. (1987) *Turning points: Treating families in transition and crisis*. New York: Norton.

Reynolds, A.L., and Pope, R.L. (1991) 'The complexities of diversity: Exploring multiple oppressions,' *Journal of Counseling & Development*, 70: 174-80.

Richardson, R., Barbour, N., & Bubenzer, D. (1991) 'Bittersweet connections: Informal social networks as sources of support and interference for adolescent mothers,' *Family Relations*, 40: 430-4.

Selvini Palazzoli, M., & Prata, G. (1982) 'Snares in family therapy,' *Journal of Marital and Family Therapy*, 8: 443-50.

Selvini Palazzoli, M., Boscolo, L., Cecchin, G., & Prata, G. (1978) *Paradox and counterparadox*. New York: Jason Aronson.

Selvini Palazzoli, M., Boscolo, L., Cecchin, G., & Prata, G. (1980) 'Hypothesizing–circularity–neutrality: Three guidelines for the conductor of the session,' *Family Process*, 19: 3-12.

Simon, R. (1972) 'Sculpting the family,' *Family Process*, 2: 49-57.

Spanier, G.B., & Glick, P.C. (1980) 'Paths to remarriage,' *Journal of Divorce*, 3: 283-98.

Todd, C.T., & Stanton, M.D. (1983) 'Research on marital and family therapy: Answers, issues, and recommendations for the future,' in B.B. Wolman & G. Stricker (eds), *Handbook of family and marital therapy*. New York: Plenum. pp. 91-115.

Tomm, K. (1988) 'Interventive interviewing: Part III. Intending to ask circular, strategic, or reflective questions?' *Family Process*, 27: 1-15.

Umbarger, C.C. (1983) *Structural family therapy*. Boston: Allyn & Bacon.

US Bureau of the Census (1990) *Marital status and living arrangements: March 1989*. (Report No. 445). Washington, DC: US Government Printing Office.

Watzlawick, P., Weakland, J.H., & Fisch, R. (1974) *Change: Principles of problem formation and problem resolution*. New York: W.W. Norton.

Weeks, G. (1977) 'Toward a dialectical approach to intervention,' *Human Development*, 20: 277-92.

Weeks, G., & L'Abate, L. (1982) *Paradoxical psychotherapy: Theory and practice with individuals, couples, and families*. New York: Brunner/Mazel.

White, M., & Epston, D. (1990) *Narrative means to therapeutic ends.* New York: W.W. Norton.

Wiener, N. (1967) *The human use of human beings: Cybernetics and society* (2nd ed.). New York: Aron.

Yalom, I.D. (1985) *The theory and practice of group psychotherapy* (3rd ed.). New York: Basic Books.

Index

Index compiled by Ann Hall